ON THE SIGNIFICANCE OF RELIGION FOR DELIBERATIVE DEMOCRACY

This exciting volume pioneers the study of the complex relationship between religion and deliberative democracy, a practice that places importance on the need for citizens to come together to identify shared concerns and issues, work through choices and options for action, weigh consequences and trade-offs, and possibly take collective action to influence decisions and policies.

Chapters use case studies to demonstrate instances where deliberative democracy has advanced the positive role of religion and where religious practices have advanced the role of deliberative democracy. The authors look at the actions of various denominations of Christianity in Africa, the United States of America, and the South Pacific, as well as examining how such groups operate within the context of indigenous religions such as African Traditional Religion. This volume also explores instances where the absence of deliberative practices in religion has curtailed the ability of people to realise their full potential, and the ability of religious groups to act decisively for the common good to influence the politics of the times.

Combining innovative research with case studies and practical implications and recommendations for religious leaders, academics, policy makers, and practitioners, this concise and easily accessible volume instructs on how religious and democratic institutions can symbiotically address community and national challenges.

Ruby Quantson Davis is a peace and development specialist, an Associate Member of Wesley House Cambridge, UK, faculty member of the Deliberative Democracy Institute, and former Fellow and Resident Scholar of the Kettering Foundation in the United States.

Elizabeth Gish is currently Program Officer at the Kettering Foundation. Previously Associate Professor, Department of Philosophy and Religion, Western Kentucky University, USA.

Kudakwashe Chitsike is a lawyer and consultant on sexual violence and global health investigation in Zimbabwe.

Religion Matters
On the Significance of Religion in Global Issues
Edited by Christine Schliesser, Zurich University / Fribourg University, Switzerland, S. Ayse Kadayifci-Orellana, Georgetown University, USA, and Pauline Kollontai, York St. John University, UK.

Policy makers, academics and practitioners worldwide are increasingly paying attention to the role of religion in global issues. This development is clearly noticeable in conflict resolution, development or climate change, to name just a few pressing issues of global relevance. Up to now, no book series has yet attempted to analyse the role of religion in current global issues in a coherent and systematic way that pertains to academics, policy makers and practitioners alike. The Sustainable Development Goals (SDGs) serve as a dynamic frame of reference. "Religion Matters" provides cutting edge scholarship in a concise format and accessible language, thereby addressing academics, practitioners and policy makers.

On the Significance of Religion for Global Diplomacy
Philip McDonagh, Kishan Manocha, John Neary, and Lucia Vázquez Mendoza

On the Significance of Religion in Violence Against Women and Girls
Elisabet le Roux and Sandra Iman Pertek

On the Significance of Religion for Deliberative Democracy
Ruby Quantson Davis, Elizabeth Gish, and Kudakwashe Chitsike

For more information about this series, please visit: https://www.routledge.com/religion/series/RELMAT

ON THE SIGNIFICANCE OF RELIGION FOR DELIBERATIVE DEMOCRACY

Ruby Quantson Davis, Elizabeth Gish, and Kudakwashe Chitsike

LONDON AND NEW YORK

Designed cover image: Regina Baumhauer: Open Letter, The Body Forgets Nothing, 2012, acrylic graphite on paper, 79 cm x 58 cm

First published 2023
by Routledge
4 Park Square, Milton Park, Abingdon, Oxon OX14 4RN

and by Routledge
605 Third Avenue, New York, NY 10158

Routledge is an imprint of the Taylor & Francis Group, an informa business

© 2023 Ruby Quantson Davis, Elizabeth Gish, and Kudakwashe Chitsike

The right of Ruby Quantson Davis, Elizabeth Gish, and Kudakwashe Chitsike to be identified as authors of this work has been asserted in accordance with sections 77 and 78 of the Copyright, Designs and Patents Act 1988.

All rights reserved. No part of this book may be reprinted or reproduced or utilised in any form or by any electronic, mechanical, or other means, now known or hereafter invented, including photocopying and recording, or in any information storage or retrieval system, without permission in writing from the publishers.

Trademark notice: Product or corporate names may be trademarks or registered trademarks, and are used only for identification and explanation without intent to infringe.

British Library Cataloguing-in-Publication Data
A catalogue record for this book is available from the British Library

ISBN: 978-1-032-10215-3 (hbk)
ISBN: 978-1-032-10216-0 (pbk)
ISBN: 978-1-003-21425-0 (ebk)

DOI: 10.4324/9781003214250

Typeset in Bembo
by codeMantra

CONTENTS

Authors		*ix*
Acknowledgements		*xi*
Abbreviations		*xv*
	Introduction: Religion and Deliberative Democracy: An Interface of Practices	1
1	Deliberative Democracy and Religion as Practices: Problems and Potentials	12
2	Case Study 1: Religious Spaces and Gender-Based Violence: A Deliberative Approach to Voicing our Pain	37
3	Case Study 2: *"Gyae ma ne nka"* (Let It Be): A Religious Notion of Peace or a Shutdown of Democratic Conversations?	70
4	Case Study 3: Church, Charity, and Philanthropy: Deciding Faith-Based Actions Democratically	98

5 Now What? Recommendations and
   Implications for Policy Makers, Religious
   Leaders, Researchers, and Practitioners   123

Index   *129*

AUTHORS

Ruby Quantson Davis is a scholar-practitioner with 20 years of global experience in public policy research and advocacy, deliberative conversations, community engagement, and institutional development. With a background in international affairs, Davis specialises in peace processes in places of polarisation and conflict. She has worked extensively within Africa, the South Pacific, Israel, and the United States, using innovative ways of reflecting, learning, documenting, and sharing knowledge. Davis currently serves as the Senior Advisor for Learning and Impact at Peace Direct, an international charity in London. She is an Associate Member of Wesley House Cambridge in the United Kingdom, serves as a faculty member of the Deliberative Democracy Institute, and is a former Fellow and Resident Scholar of the Kettering Foundation in the United States.

Elizabeth Gish studied political science and comparative religion at Miami University of Ohio and received her master's and doctoral degrees from Harvard Divinity School. From 2011 to 2020, Gish was a faculty member at the Mahurin Honors College at Western Kentucky University, where she also served as interim chair of the Department of Philosophy and Religion. In 2020, she began as a programme officer at the Kettering Foundation. Gish's research focuses on the intersection between religion and public life. She is ordained in the Christian Church (Disciples of Christ) and is active in community-building work.

Kudakwashe Chitsike is a lawyer who also serves as a consultant on a sexual violence and global health investigation in Zimbabwe. Chitsike has 20 years of experience working on human rights, democracy, and governance issues in Zimbabwe's non-governmental sector. Chitsike has documented politically motivated sexual violence against women, she has written extensively on transitional justice, governance with special emphasis on women's rights and political participation. Chitsike holds an LLM in International Public Law from Stellenbosch University and is working towards her PhD in the Department of Political and International Studies at Rhodes University in South Africa. She was an International Civil Society Fellow of the Kettering Foundation in 2005. She is an Eisenhower Fellow who completed the Women and Leadership Programme in 2015 and currently leads the Zimbabwe Chapter.

ACKNOWLEDGEMENTS

From all authors: This book is the product of cross-disciplinary, cross-cultural, and cross-organisational conversations in our various spheres of life. These conversations became the foundation for this volume in the spring of 2019 in Princeton, New Jersey, following a presentation by Ruby Quantson Davis of her research on citizens and deliberative democracy at the Center of Theological Inquiry. We are deeply grateful to Professor Pauline Kollontai and Dr. Christine Schliesser who followed up on the presentation and offered the opportunity to put a volume together as part of Routledge's *Religion Matters* series. Together with their co-series editor, Dr. Ayse Kadayifci-Orellana, these editors have guided us through the process of structuring our research, our lived and professional experiences, and our policy recommendations into a single volume. We are very grateful. We wish to thank our colleagues at the Kettering Foundation, including but not limited to Sharon Davies, David Mathews, John Dedrick, and Maxine Thomas, all of whom have influenced and been supportive of this work. We also wish to thank the Kettering Foundation research exchange participants who have met for many years to share what they are learning at the intersection of deliberative democracy and religion, and whose experiences and reflections have been essential to our research. We also thank our editors and colleagues, Amy Dragga, Marietjie Oelofsen, and Routledge editors, who went through the book critically. Additionally, we wish to thank the religious leaders and their members in various parts of the United States, Africa, and Oceania who were in conversation with us over the last several years and whose insight and guidance has helped to shape this work for the better. We wish to thank our colleagues, fellow academics, practitioners, and community leaders who shed light on the themes discussed here, granted interviews, and engaged in often difficult and time-consuming conversations. Not least, we wish to thank many friends and family who have supported us and our work.

From Elizabeth Gish: I want to thank my colleagues at Western Kentucky University, the Kettering Foundation, the Christian Church (DOC), and within Unitarian Universalism for supporting my research, teaching, and ministry. It is not possible to thank everyone by name, but I particularly wish to thank John Dedrick, Ekaterina Lukianova, Audra Jennings, Craig Cobane, Sharon Davies, David Mathews, Caroline Perrotti, Noëlle McAfee, Gregg Kaufman, Leah Schade, Derrick Hammond, David Allred, Karen Bray, Megan Huston, and Teri Schwartz. I could not have done this without the support of Sarah Taylor Peck, Rebecca Gale, Jennifer West, Erin Marsh, or my women's group and our facilitator Phil Chanin. I am always indebted to my mentors, Michael Nygren, Elisabeth Schüssler Fiorenza, and Susan Abraham. I am deeply appreciative to have been able to work on this with my brilliant and compassionate colleagues, Ruby Quantson Davis and Kudakwashe Chitsike. I am thankful for my parents, James Owen and Jan Gish, who have loved, encouraged, and supported me. I am thankful for Wolfgang, Jason, and Grace, co-parents of our little ones. And, finally, I do this work for my beloved children, living and deceased: Elijah, Victoria, Dante, Atreyu, and Amelie. And for all our children.

From Kudakwashe Chitsike: I would like to thank the women I have interviewed over the years for trusting me with their experiences of sexual violence. It is not an easy topic to discuss with a stranger; I respectfully honour all of you. I am very grateful to my family, especially my parents, Bisset Cosmas Chitsike, who was a deeply religious man, a writer, and an editor, and my mother,

Annah Colletah Chitsike, a gender activist. Together they cultivated a reading, writing, and learning culture that resulted in my co-authoring this book. Thank you to my sister, Takudzwa, for the words of support and encouragement when things became tough. To my friends—Tambudzai Madzimure, Tsitsi Dzinevane, and Melody Sango—sisters from other mothers, thank you for believing in me when I was overthinking and faltering. I would like to thank the Kettering Foundation for bringing Ruby Quantson Davis and I together as International Civil Society Fellows in 2005. This book is Ruby's brainchild: we talked about it for years and you made it happen and together with Dr. Elizabeth Gish, a minister and a scholar, co-authored this book. I am honoured to work with you both.

From Ruby Quantson Davis: To my co-authors, Elizabeth Gish and Kuda Chitsike, thank you for your superb ability to process this book idea, and for your commitment to its realisation within the uncertainties of a global pandemic. I am grateful for the learning spaces offered by my colleagues in the Faculty of the Deliberative Democracy Institute, led by Maxine Thomas, and the International Network of the Kettering Foundation, comprising amazing "workers of democracy" in over 50 countries. I thank all organisations and persons with whom I have worked over the years for shaping my ideas on international development and the global power imbalances that have necessitated the chapters in this book. To theologians, Dr. Angela Dwamena-Aboagye in Ghana, and Professor Dion Forster in South Africa, thanks for taking the time to talk through your work with me; our conversations have impacted this volume immensely. I am grateful for the support of my family, particularly my parents, who, as public servants in Ghana, taught us to recognise the call to duty: my mum, Comfort Ardayfio, who is an example of how the Church and its congregants can transform everyday lives, and my dad, Kofi Quantson, Esq., who as senior public official and as a prolific writer, has no doubt inculcated reading and writing in me; my husband, Dr. Richard A. Davis, whose love for academic excellence, and "all things books" encouraged this work to continue; and to his parents, Pam and Arthur, for supporting my work with insightful ideas. To my siblings and friends far and wide, conversations with you have shaped the ideas in this book and for that I am truly grateful.

Cover photo: Regina Baumhauer
Open Letter, The Body Forgets Nothing, 2012;
acrylic graphite on paper;
79 cm × 58 cm
http://www.suedwestgalerie.de/regina-baumhauer/kunstwerk/5188

ABBREVIATIONS

ATR:	African Traditional Religion
CEDAW:	Convention on the Elimination of All Forms of Discrimination Against Women
GBV:	gender-based violence
GMC:	Global Methodist Church
HIV:	human immunodeficiency virus
MDC:	Movement for Democratic Change
NAACP:	National Association for the Advancement of Colored People
NGOs	non-governmental organisations
NRSV:	New Revised Standard Version
PTSD:	post-traumatic stress disorder
SDGs:	Sustainable Development Goals
STIs:	sexually transmitted infections
UDHR:	Universal Declaration of Human Rights
UMC:	United Methodist Church
US:	United States
ZANU–PF:	Zimbabwe African National Union–Patriotic Front
ZDHS:	Zimbabwe Demographic and Health Survey
ZIMSTAT:	Zimbabwe National Statistics Agency

Summary Recommendations and Implications for Policy Makers, Religious Leaders, Researchers and Practitioners

Religious organisations can develop and share meaningful democratic spaces with other development actors to advance the common good. Deliberation as a democratic practice aligns with several religious practices, including but not limited to acting on complex social and moral issues, and working together with others. If fully explored, such efforts will provide more responsive, inclusive, participatory, and representative decision-making at all levels, in line with United Nations Sustainable Development Goals (SDGs) 16 and 17. This can help to address the ambivalence of religion in several critical injustices in society.

Implication One: Redefining Politics to Embrace Everyday Choices

If "politics" is reframed to describe the choice work that citizens have to engage in order to make or influence decisions that affect their well-being, everyday people are more likely to engage the issues highlighted in the SDGs. Religious spaces, which tend to attract large gatherings of citizens in the places studied in this book, are important spaces to demystify conversations around development and encourage citizen engagement.

Implication Two: The Need for Cross-Fertilisation of Ideas among Religious Groups

It is useful for religious leaders to create platforms for mutual learning exchanges. Ecumenical and interfaith/multifaith platforms can enable cross-fertilisation of ideas. Similarly, practitioners and researchers of deliberative democracy can make concrete efforts to expose religious groups to democratic practices that align with religious practices. When people work together to find solutions to common problems, they are more likely to find their mutual interests and recognise their common humanity.

Implication Three: Intersectoral Collaboration and Learning

To explore the potentials at the interface of religious and democratic practices, the gaps among academics, researchers, civic groups, religious organisations, and policy makers ought to be narrowed. Cooperation ought to occur at inception and conceptualisation stages of programmes to help gather insights from various groups. The deliberative practices proposed in this book provide structure and focus for such conversations to generate useful and collective outcomes.

Implication Four: Build on Local Epistemologies and Traditional Practices

Different or alternative systems of learning, knowledge and ways of engagement from different parts of the world ought to be surfaced to foster greater collaboration between diverse groups. It is important to ask not just who is missing, but also whose epistemology is obscured, downplayed, or deliberately eliminated. People get disempowered when they are forced to use knowledge systems that are foreign to their own daily existence and experiences. This must form part of the decolonisation agenda and a locally led development agenda.

Implication Five: Women's Voices in Decision-Making

Given that violence against women is often justified by traditional and religious texts, religious groups have an obligation to do more to change the way these texts are interpreted in their contexts. Heads of religious institutions, committees, associations, and guilds have an essential role to play. Supported by feminist and womanist readings of sacred texts, positive cultural norms, and deliberative spaces, religious leaders can provide safer spaces for women to seek support, inform policies, and actively take on empowering roles. Changes in gender narratives within religious communities can go a long way to influence state and national policies.

Implication Six: Charities and Policy Influence

Charitable activities and philanthropic efforts can take people from dependence on charities to greater self-sufficiency and sustainability. One approach to this is to involve recipients in the decisions that affect them, and to ultimately seek to transform the division between recipients and givers. This gives those who are typically recipients of help the opportunity to name the problem in ways that are meaningful to them. This is enabling and empowering. It also offers givers the opportunity to learn and work collaboratively to achieve the SDGs. A shift in the way charity is understood and carried out can sustainably improve livelihoods.

Implication Seven: Theological Appraisal and Training

Periodic theological appraisal of religious and democratic practices within specific cultural contexts, guided by improved humanitarian frameworks (such as the SDGs), should inform which religious practices are worth upholding and those that should be modified or discarded. This requires consistent capacity development for faithful people, church leaders, and workers. Based on the cases discussed in this book, some of the skills-upgrading and knowledge-building required should be on: (1) issue identification; (2) framing, creating, and facilitating deliberative spaces; (3) mediation; (4) promoting effective and just collective action; (5) mental health support; and (6) leadership.

INTRODUCTION

Religion and Deliberative Democracy: An Interface of Practices

There is significant interconnectedness between religion and social, economic, and cultural life. Berger and Neuhaus (2021) cite congregations as an example of a mediating structure; that is, those institutions that stand between an individual's "private" life and large institutions of public life. In places like Western Europe and in some contexts in the United States, religion is conceived to be in the realm of the private. In many other regions, including Africa and Oceania, religion is less separated from the traditions and everyday lives of people. Metaphors, proverbs, and statements for admonishing society are deeply intertwined in traditional and religious practices. Across Africa, the church has been a source of support and cause of upheavals in democratic movements (Gifford 1998). Christianity in sub-Saharan Africa has been seen, at times, as an ideology of hegemonic control as well as a vehicle for community mobilisation (Haynes 2007). Such mobilisation may not always look political. This is because it draws on cultural creativity as well as spiritual and religious symbolism (Ranger 1986), revealing the interconnectivity between religion and culture and their impact on everyday lives. A shared sense of justice and a search

DOI: 10.4324/9781003214250-1

for the common good drives this engagement between religion and democracy, a collective ethic already present in many parts of communitarian societies such as Africa (Gyekye 1997; Chaplin 2021). This provides religion a place and potentially the tools—which they generate themselves and in cooperation with democratic institutions—to address pressing community and national challenges.

For religion to sustainably address the growing global challenges, the interconnectivity between religious matters and people's everyday lives ought to surface. However, the perception of "they and us", as well as rigid rules of religious practice, has often limited the spaces for religion to engage community or serve as the grounds to nurture community building and collective action. For some, it is hard to imagine how a religious space can consider divergent views and offer a space for acting collectively with others of different persuasions and world views without evangelisation. Such perception and limitations have excluded many people, and ultimately diminished the capacity of religious organisations to create democratically active congregations and communities that can produce public goods—tangible and intangible. In other contexts, religion and matters of faith are delinked from public discourses. As Jonathan Chaplin observes in *Faith in Democracy*, "the sooner we all put behind us the illusion that public debate can be governed by a detached 'objectivity'—'a view from nowhere'—the more likely we are to edge towards mutual understanding; or, at least, towards better disagreement" (2021: xvii). The author further posits that unless religious organisations engage people in ways that resonate and directly affect the lives of the people, the positive significance of religion in everyday lives will not be fully realised. How can such an interface occur productively?

This book suggests that deliberation can be a democratic practice by which religion can engage with pressing needs and contribute to peace and well-being at the family, neighbourhood, community, national, and international levels. If religious organisations create meaningful democratic spaces where concerns and divergent views are expressed and negotiated, conflicts are likely to be averted or at least managed, relationships strengthened, and the common good could be carried out collectively while significantly reducing civic apathy. Religious institutions can begin to be "safe houses". Our effort is not to have religious groups insert themselves into existing democratic systems (Chaplin 2021). As highlighted above, religion and democracy inevitably interact in many ways and therefore need not be at odds with each other in a zero-sum game (ibid.). As this book demonstrates, in many ways, there is more alignment in practices and goals than has been previously explored. The task, then, is how to navigate obligations of citizenship and the demands of faith. While there will be tensions in this interaction, we will be worse off if we attempted to construct a system in which the two did not interact.

In this volume, our authors explore the complex relationship between religion and deliberative democracy, a practice that places importance on the need for citizens to come together to identify shared concerns and issues, work through choices and options for action, weigh consequences and trade-offs, and possibly take collective action (Mathews 2014). A central question of this work is *how* citizens act as democratic beings to shape the world in which they live. A key objective of the volume is to demonstrate instances where deliberative democracy has advanced the positive role of religion and where religious practices have advanced the role of deliberative democracy. We show how religion can benefit from deliberative democratic practices, and the ways deliberative democracy can be enriched by careful attention to its role in, and relationship with, religious life. We also explore instances where the absence of deliberative practices in religion has limited the ability of people to realise their full potential, and the ability of religious groups to act for the common good to influence the political and development challenges of our times.

This work highlights the role that deliberative practices can play in allowing religious institutions to achieve the potential they have and to carry out the role in society that so many religious organisations claim that they wish to play, while at the same time addressing the problems arising from religious traditions in view of deliberative and democratic practices (Bloom and Arikan 2013). When religious groups integrate deliberative democratic practices into the life of their community, it better enables them to see and honour the full humanity of those within the religious community and address shared problems together. These practices also improve the deliberative habits and skills of those who take part, thus strengthening democratic institutions outside of religious contexts. In this book, we highlight how religious contexts can provide important sites for democratic deliberation and reform, even as religion has colluded in violence, particularly violence against women. In many ways, the book highlights some of the barriers to deliberation within the scope of religion and conflicts of theology. As Chaplin (2021) suggests, it is better for religion and democracy to interact, and even engage in disagreements, in facilitated, well-framed and principled spaces, than to operate apart. Such engagements create room for "broad political consensus on important matters of public policy" (ibid: xiii).

Theorists and practitioners understand deliberative democracy in various ways. While the term was popularised by Habermas (1998), it is understood more broadly in the literature today (Carcasson and Sprain 2016). For the purposes here, deliberation is distinct from dialogue and civil conversation in that it includes, but goes beyond, respectful listening and increased understanding. It also involves sharing reasons, weighing trade-offs, making choices, and identifying common ground for action. Deliberative democracy certainly can include electoral politics, but also goes well beyond elections to include everyday actions of citizens outside of institutions and government (Kinney 2012; Leighninger 2006). While drawing from and engaging in the theoretical debates on deliberative democracy, this book focuses on what deliberative democracy looks like on the ground and *how* religion intersects with, influences, and is influenced by, deliberative democracy in various contexts, cultures, and practices.

The conceptual and methodological basis for the book begins with an acknowledgement of the complex and ambivalent history of religion. There is ample and painful evidence that religion can do a significant amount of harm (Blackburn 2004; Colpe 2008; Cone 1974). We also acknowledge that deliberative democracy is not without its challenges and is certainly not a panacea for the challenges of shared "life together" (Bonhoeffer 2009), religious or secular. That said, we do believe that both religion and deliberative democracy have the potential to contribute to the common good and we take this as our starting point. This book seeks a balance between clearly acknowledging the harm that religious institutions and people can and have caused, while, at the same time, naming and fostering the potential for religious practices and institutions to contribute to stronger, healthier, and more just communities as per the SDGs (United Nations 2015).

This volume finds expression in the 16th SDG. Target 16.7 calls for "responsive, inclusive, participatory and representative decision-making at all levels". Target 16.8 highlights the need to "broaden and strengthen the participation of developing countries in the institutions of global governance", hence the inclusion of a number of cases from developing countries in this volume. These are also countries in regions where religious beliefs are vibrantly upheld and religion mobilises a large part of the population.

The volume is also situated within the framework of "co-production". Political economist and Nobel laureate Elinor Ostrom has described co-production as a process in which officials see citizens as producers (and citizens act as such) to produce public goods. This volume, like others in the series, is designed to encourage a multi-sectoral approach to addressing development issues and foster collaboration between policy makers and other actors such as citizens, practitioners, academics, and certainly religious leaders.

This work also builds on insights from feminist and womanist theories that argue that research is "always perspectival and sociopolitically situated" (Schüssler Fiorenza 2011: 58; Townes 2006). In "Re-Visioning Christian Origins: *In Memory of Her* Revisited", feminist New Testament scholar Elisabeth Schüssler Fiorenza reminds readers that scholarship always "produces knowledge that sustain[s] either domination or emancipation" (2003: 225–250). Given this, research cannot be neutral. The work here is not disinterested. The authors are all committed—vocationally, religiously, and ethically—to a world where people are able to live well among each other, where people work together to create more just communities, and where equality and well-being are prioritised.

We began this project not with a hypothesis that we sought to confirm or deny, but rather with data gathered in the course of our collective professions and lived experiences. Such data has been gathered through observation, interviews, stories, and ethnographic research that centres the lived experience of everyday people (Babbitt 1993; Charmaz 2014). In conversation with the existing literature, this allowed us to move towards tentative conclusions. With these tentative conclusions, we then looped back to experiences, observations, and practices that are being carried out in communities. It has been an iterative process that rejects static findings in lieu of a focus on learning, reflection, and co-production of knowledge. Additionally, rather than burying the connections "between self and other and between the personal and political" (Grinenko Baker 2005: 22), we foreground these tensions and connections, understanding that all scholars bring their experiences and histories to their work whether or not they are explicit about this. It is our intention that this helps the readers to contextualise our research and to recognise the importance of their own experiences, histories, and practices as they approach this area of study.

This book is a shift from most of the writing at the intersection of religion and deliberative democracy, often framed as "the problem of religion". This approach asks: can or should citizens bring their religious beliefs and realities to public deliberation? Is this a legitimate source of reasoning? If not, how is this to be controlled or prevented? And if so, how should this be handled and understood alongside secular beliefs that are often presumed to be grounded in reason (Lafont 2009; March and Steinmetz 2018)? Additionally, at a deeper level, there is also the problem of the democracy-fitness of religion (e.g., patriarchy, hierarchy, power structures).

Although the above conversations are important, this volume rather considers the resonances that deliberative democracy and religious practices/theologies have with each other, or the ways that they can be mutually enhancing. The book uniquely draws examples from diverse ethno-religious contexts to engage the complex significance of religion and deliberative democracy. The book takes a close insider's look at the actions of various denominations and sects of Christianity in Africa and the United States, with particular attention to the role of African Traditional Religion (ATR) in African Christian contexts. This perspective and approach will appeal to large populations because it resonates with the intertwined nature of their religious practices and daily lived experiences.

Outline of the book

This volume is organised around four chapters. It begins with summary recommendations and an introduction, and ends with a set of recommendations for various stakeholders including policy makers, religious entities, and civil society organisations.

Chapter one, "Deliberative Democracy and Religion as Practices: Problems and Potentials", outlines the theoretical framework and key themes of the book. It explores the application of democratic deliberation in faith contexts to help people work through tensions at the intersection of difficult religious and political issues. This chapter surfaces the synergy between democratic practices and religious practices and presents religious groups as key actors in solving development challenges and as collaborators towards the realisation of the SDGs.

Chapters two, three, and four are presented as case studies to demonstrate the potential and problems discussed in Chapter one.

Chapter two, "Religious Spaces and Gender-Based Violence: A Deliberative Approach to Voicing our Pain", explores the ambivalence of religion in the context of gender-based violence in Zimbabwe. Drawing examples from ATR and Christianity, this chapter suggests that deliberative spaces in religious organisations, particularly where women often form the largest part of the congregation, can be fertile ground for addressing societal issues such as violence against women.

Chapter three, is titled "*Gyae ma ne nka* (Let it be): A Religious Notion of Peace or a Shut-down of Democratic Conversations?" In many cultures such as in Africa and Oceania, notions of *Gyae ma ne nka* (an Akan expression), often framed as forgiveness in the context of Christianity, are intended to promote peaceful co-existence and social cohesion. However, if it is invoked without the necessary spaces and interventions for addressing grievances, the concept could promote injustice, silence people, and threaten the peace of the individual (a victim) and the stability of communities. This chapter proposes fostering deliberative spaces in religion as a healthier approach to realising the intent behind *gyae ma ne nka* and to advance peace and stability.

Chapter four, "Church, Charity, and Philanthropy: Deciding Faith-Based Actions Democratically", looks at the role that deliberative democratic practices can play in helping churches and other religious organisations understand themselves as part of addressing shared concerns, rather than as saviours for "others" in need. The chapter suggests that religious organisations can engage in conversations and actions that could tackle the root causes of the problems they seek to address through their outreach and mission programmes. Deliberations that lead to identifying a common ground for action can help build a shared understanding of the issues and provide more comprehensive and sustainable solutions to the shared challenges of life together.

References

Babbitt, Susan. (1993). "Feminism and Objective Interests? The Role of Transformation Experiences in Rational Deliberation," in Linda Alcoff and Elizabeth Potter (eds.), *Feminist Epistemologies*. New York: Routledge, 245–264.

Bloom, Ben-Nun Pazit, and Arikan, Gizem. (2013). "Religion and Support for Democracy: A Cross-National Test of the Mediating Mechanisms", *British Journal of Political Science*, 43(2): 375–397. doi: 10.1017/S0007123412000427.

Bloom, Ben-Nun Pazit, and Arikan, Gizem. (2012). "Priming Religious Belief and Religious Social Behavior Affects Support for Democracy", *International Journal of Public Opinion Research*, 25(3), 368–382. doi: 10.1093/ijpor/eds030.

Berger, Peter, and Neuhaus, Richard. (2021). "To Empower People: The Role of Mediating Structures in Public Policy", in J. Steven Ott and Lisa Dicke (eds.), *Nature of the Nonprofit Sector*. New York: Routledge, 350–361.

Blackburn, Carole. (2004). *Harvest of Souls: The Jesuit Missions and Colonialism in North America, 1632–1650*. Montreal: McGill-Queen's University Press.

Bonhoeffer, Dietrich. (2009). *Life Together*. New York: HarperOne.

Carcasson, Martín, and Sprain, Leah. (2016). "Beyond Problem Solving: Reconceptualizing the Work of Public Deliberation as Deliberative Inquiry", *Communication Theory*, 26(1): 41–63. doi.org/10.1111/comt.12055.

Chambers, Simone. (2003). "Deliberative Democratic Theory", *Annual Review of Political Science*, 6(1): 307–326. doi.org/10.1146/annurev.polisci.6.121901.085538.

Chaplin, Jonathan. (2021). *Faith in Democracy: Framing a Politics of Deep Diversity*. London: SCM Press.

Charmaz, Kathy. (2014). *Constructing Grounded Theory* (2nd ed.). Thousand Oaks, CA: Sage Publications.

Colpe, Carsten. (2008). "Xenophobia", in Erwin Fahlbusch, Jan Milič Lochman, John Mbiti, Jaroslav Pelikan and Lukas Vischer (eds.), *Encyclopedia of Christianity*, vol. 5. Leiden Netherlands: Brill.

Cone, James. (1974). *A Black Theology of Liberation*. Philadelphia, PA: Lippincott.

Djupe, Paul, and Calfano, Brian. (2012). "The Deliberative Pulpit? The Democratic Norms and Practices of the PCUSA", *Journal for the Scientific Study of Religion*, 51(1): 90–109. www.jstor.org/stable/41349930.

Djupe, Paul, and Olson, Laura. (2013). "Public Deliberation about Gay Rights in Religious Contexts: Commitment to Deliberative Norms and Practice in ELCA Congregations", *Journal of Public Deliberation*, 9(1). doi.org/10.16997/jdd.150.

Frawley-O'Dea, Mary Gail and Goldner, Virginia (eds.). (2016). *Predatory Priests, Silenced Victims: The Sexual Abuse Crisis and the Catholic Church*. New York: Routledge.

Gifford, Paul. (1998). *African Christianity: It's Public Role*. London: Hurst and Company.

Gish, Elizabeth. (2020). "Toward the World We Long For: Churches and the Hope of Democratic Life", *eJournal of Public Affairs*, 9(2). www.ejournalofpublicaffairs.org/toward-the-world-we-long-for-churches-and-the-hope-of-democratic-life/.

Grinenko Baker, Dori. (2005). *Doing Girlfriend Theology: God-Talk with Young Women*. Cleveland, OH: The Pilgrim Press.

Gyekye, Kwame. (1997). *Tradition and Modernity: Philosophical Reflections on the African Experience*. Oxford: Oxford University Press.

Habermas, Jürgen. (1998). *Between Facts and Norms: Contributions to a Discourse Theory of Law and Democracy*. Cambridge, MA: MIT Press.

Haynes, Jeff. (2004). "Religion and Democratization in Africa", *Democratization*, 11(4), 66–89. doi.org/10.1080/1351034042000234530.

Kinney, Bo. (2012). "Deliberation's Contribution to Community Capacity Building", in Tina Nabatchi, John Gastil, Matt Leighninger, and G. Michael Weiksner (eds.), *Democracy in Motion: Evaluating the Practice and Impact of Deliberative Civic Engagement*. New York: Oxford University Press.

Lafont, Cristina. (2009). "Religion and the Public Sphere: What are the Deliberative Obligations of Democratic Citizenship?" *Philosophy & Social Criticism*, 35(1–2): 127–150. doi.org/10.1177/0191453708098758.

Leighninger, Matt. (2006). *The Next Form of Democracy: How Expert Rule is Giving Way to Shared Governance—and Why Politics Will Never Be the Same*. Nashville, TN: Vanderbilt University Press.

March, Andrew and Steinmetz, Alicia. (2018). "Religious Reasons in Public Deliberation", in Andre Bächtiger, John Dryzek, Jane Mansbridge, and Mark Warren (eds.), *Oxford Handbook of Deliberative Democracy*. New York: Oxford University Press: 203–217.

Mathews, David. (2014). *The Ecology of Democracy: Finding Ways to Have a Stronger Hand in Shaping Our Future*. Dayton, OH: Kettering Foundation Press.

Neiheisel, Jacob, Djupe, Paul, and Sokhey, Anand. (2009). "Veni, Vidi, Disseri: Churches and the Promise of Democratic Deliberation", *American Politics Research*, 37(4), 614–643. doi.org/10.1177/1532673X08324216.

Ostrom, Elinor. (1993). "Covenanting, Co-Producing, and the Good Society", *Newsletter of PEGS*, 3(2): 7–9. www.jstor.org/stable/20710607.

Pierce, Gregory Augustine. (1984). *Activism that Makes Sense: Congregations and Community Organization*. Chicago: ACTA Publications.

Ranger, Terence O. (1986). "Religious Movements and Politics in Sub-Saharan Africa", *African Studies Review* 29(2) 1–69. https://doi.org/10.2307/523964.

Schüssler Fiorenza, Elisabeth. (2011). *Transforming Vision: Explorations in Feminist The*ology*. Minneapolis, MN: Fortress Press.

Townes, Emilie. (2006). *Womanist Ethics and the Cultural Production of Evil*. New York: Palgrave Macmillan.

United Nations. (2015). Sustainable Development Goals. Viewed from www.un.org/sustainabledevelopment [Date accessed October 1, 2021].

Young, Iris Marion. (1999). "Justice, Inclusion, and Deliberative Democracy", in Stephen Macedo (ed.), *Deliberative Politics: Essays on Democracy and Disagreement*. New York: Oxford University Press.

1
DELIBERATIVE DEMOCRACY AND RELIGION AS PRACTICES

Problems and Potentials

1.1 Introduction

The chapter explores the prospects and challenges when deliberative democratic practices and religious practices interface. We argue that democratic deliberation can be effectively used in faith contexts to help people work through tensions at the intersection of difficult religious and political issues. This chapter discusses deliberation as a practice by which issues can be identified and framed to be inclusive, collaborative, and action-oriented while considering the challenges in realising these aspirations within, or in collaboration with, organised religion. We highlight synergies between deliberative democratic practices and religious practices to demonstrate how and why religious groups are often well-placed to address development challenges. To address these challenges, religious groups and individuals who are part of faith communities need to practice in the "civic gym" to build the "muscles" required for effective community and global impact.

1.2 Centring Practices and Experience

Religion can define who someone is, it can refer to what they do, and it can be about what they believe. For many, it is a mix of these, and can vary both within and across traditions. Likewise, democracy can be understood in various ways. While many might begin with understanding democracy as a system of governance, there is more to the story. Living in a democracy, or not, can shape one's understanding of both their personal and collective identities. Democracy can also be understood as something people do, encompassing a range of practices such as voting, making decisions together, identifying resources to address challenges, and acting together (Mathews 2014: 119–120). Here, we follow Benjamin Barber's *Strong Democracy: Participatory Politics for a New Age* in embracing a vision of democracy that is centred on the role of everyday people as the central actors and agents in a democracy (1984).

In this book, there is a focus on religion and democracy as practices: as something people *do*. This does not imply that religion and democracy cannot legitimately and productively be understood otherwise, but rather this lens highlights the role that everyday people have in shaping the world in which they live, and in improving themselves and their communities. Throughout the text we often use "everyday people" and "citizens" interchangeably. While "citizen" can mean a member of a state, historically, there is a broader definition of citizen that emphasises a "distinctive civic ideal and set of practices involving creative agency and a form of loyalty—a commitment to a civic minded co-creation" (Boyte et al. 2009). While recognising the limitations on how "citizen" is understood in various national and cultural contexts, it is the latter understanding of citizen that we embrace in this book. By focusing on democracy and religion as formational practices, we are bringing attention to the ways that everyday people—citizens in the most inclusive sense of the word—are acting *in* the world, are acting *on* the world, and may transform both self and world.

Our emphasis on practices is guided by the French sociologist Pierre Bourdieu's theory of practice and Kathy Charmaz's work on constructivist grounded theory (Charmaz 2014). Additionally, as noted in the introduction, our work is deeply influenced both by feminist and womanist theories which emphasise the importance of experience as epistemologically significant, and the subjectivity of knowledge (Hennessy 1993: 67–99; Townes 2006).

Bourdieu developed two ideas that highlight the importance of a focus on practices. The first is the concept of *habitus*, which he characterised as "systems of durable, transposable dispositions, structured structures predisposed to function as structuring structures" embodied as "principles which generate and organise practices and representations" (Bourdieu 1990: 53). He argued that the things individuals do (i.e., practices) structure the *habitus*—in essence, they shape and structure who we are. In this light, we can understand practices such as deliberation, hospitality, discipleship, loving your neighbours, and learning together, as shaping the *habitus*—the structures that structure who we are and how we operate in the world.

This focus on what we do applies to what we do with our hands, our feet, and our bodies. Who and where do we serve? How do we treat our neighbours? Do we enact violence with our bodies? Do we use our bodies to protect those who are vulnerable? We can also think of speaking as a potentially religious, democratic, and bodily practice that shapes our *habitus*. For whom do we pray? Do we speak up for justice even when it is a risk to our bodies? Do we use language to collaborate? To alienate? Using a feminist lens to understand voice and speech highlights the way that language is a reflexive and dynamic process. It both reflects the way people experience and understand the world and, at the same time, shapes the speaker and the world, creating or limiting the possibilities for certain types of subjectivities.

In addition to his concept of *habitus*, Bourdieu wrote about the ways that humans get a "feel for the game" in their social interactions (Bourdieu 1977: 10–13; Bourdieu 1990: 27, 66–68, 82, 103). He does not use "game" in a playful sense here, but in the sense that there is not just a field of play, a set of rules and limits, but that there is room for creativity, complexity, interaction, freedom, and a certain ability to push against and challenge the rules of the game. Consider, for instance, an actual game such as basketball. Reading or thinking about the game can only take a player so far. One only learns to play well by actually playing the game, where, over time, one develops a "feel" for it through practice. Essential to this practice is that people practise alongside others. We cannot get a "feel" for the game of basketball only by playing alone. Both democracy and religion can be understood similarly. People can read about working together across differences or showing hospitality, but ultimately these efforts take practice(s)—getting a "feel for the game" as we play with others. Bourdieu's concept of *habitus* and "feel for the game" provide helpful frameworks for understanding democratic and religious practices and their formational potential, not just for the individual but also for communities and larger societies.

1.3 On Harmful Practices and Life-Giving Practices

There is ample and painful evidence that religious institutions and people can do a significant amount of harm. Churches and faith-based organisations have a long history of perpetuating sexism, racism, colonialism, xenophobia, and abuse. Additionally, many people and groups have experienced mental and physical harm, trauma, and pain when they have not conformed to worldviews, belief systems, governance structures, cultural expectations, and/or sexual/sex/gender norms that a particular religion or religious group believes to be correct. There are countless examples of religious organisations wreaking havoc on the communities in which they are situated, including lands they have invaded or communities they have entered under false pretenses. On a macro scale, we can remember, as just one instance, the genocide in what is now North and South America. European colonisers, under the banner of Christianity, seized both the land and resources while raping and killing millions of Indigenous people who lived there. Still today, we continue to see missionaries from predominantly White countries raise millions of dollars each year so that they may travel to and live in countries where the population is predominantly poor and not predominantly White, so that they may spread their version of Christianity in places that they perceive to be in great need. Within our own countries, too, we see religious organisations continue to prevent women from serving in leadership roles, and to ban sexual and gender minorities from leadership roles. While there are, of course, examples of religious people doing important, meaningful, and respectful work, the list of transgressions and harm done in the name of religion could, and in fact does, fill books. It is important to be clear-headed about the complex and mixed track record of religion as a force for good, justice, or healing.

Yet, within this clear-headed honesty about the mixed past and present of religion, it is also important to acknowledge that faith communities have provided, and continue to provide, a context for growth, healing, hope, fellowship, and connection to the divine in ways that are enriching and life-giving. The work of missionaries has helped to provide education, healthcare, and economic support to many communities around the world. The Black Church in the United States was at the centre of the Civil Rights Movement. Mahatma Gandhi, a devout Hindu, was a central figure in promoting interfaith understanding and the doctrine of non-violence. Although many televangelists have been accused of promoting self-centred prosperity gospel, Prophet T. B. Joshua, the Nigerian televangelist and founder of The Synagogue, Church of All Nations (SCOAN), was revered in many parts of Africa and the world as he provided both physical and spiritual nourishment to those in need. On a more local level, day in and day out, we can observe the ways that people are comforted in their grief, inspired by sermons, fed by food pantries, and find welcome and grace in a religious context, often when the secular world has failed them. Faith can provide ground for hope and space for the imagination of something different when humans fail to find this or provide it to each other in the temporal world.

Our focus on practices allows us to decentre what people say, what they believe, or what they intend—and to focus instead on what they do and the consequences of those actions. This does not mean ignoring belief or intention, but rather brings attention to the consequences of beliefs and intention. This approach enables us to engage a broader conversation around practices and their impact on community and global development.

Many churches and faith-based organisations have a deep commitment to the well-being of the communities where they are located and wish for things to "be better" or to "help improve things". Often, the issues that churches name as important issues overlap with the UN's SDGs. Examples include poverty, housing, hunger, the environment, inequality, safety, and security. Yet, despite efforts, many religious communities and religious institutions continue to struggle to make progress on such issues. For instance, even though there is more than enough food available in the world to feed the world's population, hunger remains a pressing problem not only in underresourced countries but also in countries, such as the United States, where lack of access to nutritious, affordable food is widespread. Wealth inequality continues to grow both within countries, as well as on a global scale (World Inequality Database 2022). Despite slogans about peace, hospitality, belonging, and welcome, the plight of refugees worldwide has continued to worsen. According to the UN High Commissioner for Refugees, the number of people who have been forcibly displaced worldwide because of persecution, conflict, violence, or human rights violations since 2008 has more than doubled (UNHCR 2021). While churches and faith groups do make sincere efforts to address these urgent issues of well-being that are theologically important to them, progress is often slow or non-existent in part because change would require costs that many individuals, faith-based organisations, and faith groups are not willing to bear. In other instances, these organisations simply do not know how to address the issues.

We know, of course, that good intentions are not enough. This study is thus intended to offer insight about how religious communities and their development partners can find ways to reduce the harm that faith groups have caused, *and* to identify approaches that will allow them to make better progress towards creating stronger, healthier, peaceful, and more just communities in line with their theological commitments.

Throughout our research, we have identified several resonances between life-giving democratic practices and life-giving practices in faith communities. These insights have emerged from interviews, informal conversations, field work, and our own scholar-practitioner engagement:

- In many democratic and religious practices, there is an emphasis on pausing to reflect and decentring the self in order

to see or hear other ways of improving ourselves. There is a shared sense that "we" do not have all the answers ourselves, and however encoded some answers are (in scripture or law), they remain incomplete.
- There is an acknowledgment that whatever we are doing has to relate to something that we already have: what we are doing cannot be completely disconnected from what has gone before.
- There is a sense that our work and efforts are proximate or open-ended. There is always uncertainty, and the story is neither closed nor ever fully known.
- Finally, there is a sense that humanity cannot thrive or be complete without community.

In writing about democratic politics and religious work in *Resurrecting Democracy: Faith, Citizenship and the Politics of a Common Life*, Luke Bretherton reminds his readers that democratic politics "does not offer salvation", but for those in religious contexts, "it can provide some consolation for and a way of coping with the grief of living between the world as it is and as it should be" (285). It is helpful to acknowledge that, with our efforts will also come grief—a sense that things are still not as they should be and that there is more to be done. Yet, recognising the ways that both democratic and religious practices can be mutually reinforcing serves as a reminder. We see how our political and religious longings often spring from similar places as we struggle to live well with and among each other. To engage in this work is to engage in a journey towards the world we long for, and it is also to hope that things might be other than they are. Holding these tensions well—the challenge of acting and also the hope of transformation—is at the heart of this work.

1.4 Deliberation in Everyday Politics

Often, a distinction is drawn between religious activities and political activities. The US tax code affirms this distinction, limiting the ways that churches engage in political activities to maintain their tax-exempt status. In Zimbabwe, when churches speak out against the government, they are reminded of the distinction between religion and politics and told to stay in their own sphere, as was the case when Catholic bishops wrote a pastoral letter accusing the Zimbabwean government of human rights abuses in August 2020. Sometimes, it is possible and productive to delineate religious identity, belief, and practices on the one hand, and political identity, belief, and practices on the other. For instance, the distinction between religious conviction and legal expectations has helped protect many in the United States and elsewhere from being subject to the religious expectations of their fellow citizens. Yet, in many ways, the political and the religious are inextricable. Democratic theorists have highlighted the ways that political life stretches beyond formal or institutional politics with terms like *everyday politics* (Boyte 2005) and *organic politics* (Mathews 2014). Similarly, Bayat's (2012) *Life as Politics* offered important insights into an understanding of politics that takes seriously the way everyday actions by citizens meaningfully shape possibilities for shared existence. Understood this way, citizens take part in political life not only when they vote, protest, or campaign, but also when they give money to people in need, care for children, discuss the value of human life at a Bible study, post on social media, or respond to a complicated interpersonal situation at work. Politics is not simply who gets what, when, and how; it is about how we live together among each other, day in and day out.

The ways religious and political beliefs, identities, and practices cannot be fully separated are underlined by the popular refrain that emerged from second-wave feminist movements: "The personal is political". Initially, the phrase referred to the ways that certain actions often rendered "personal" (e.g., cleaning the house, taking care of children) had implications that necessarily reached beyond individuals' lives and structured possibilities for shared existence. This refrain resonates today as many people struggle to make sense of the implications our everyday actions and decisions have—not only for our own communities and neighbours, but also for people across the world whose lives are bound up with our own through systems of culture, governance, and commerce. Given this, the work here treats the political work of faith groups broadly, beyond engagement in electoral politics, and includes the ways those within faith groups engage with each other and their neighbours, how they develop policies, and how they interact with the local, national, and global communities in which they are situated. In its ideal form, we envision that democratic deliberation becomes a relational habit that spans the political and religious—a way of acting and learning together that is woven into the fabric of communities.

In some cases, when people deliberate, they use guides or frameworks to guide the process. The National Issues Forums Institute (NIFI) has produced hundreds of guides on topics ranging from racism to hunger, from end-of-life care to bullying (www.nifi.org). Tens of thousands of people have used the guides across the world, and they are available in Spanish, Russian, English, and Hebrew. Many communities also develop their own deliberative guides to help frame difficult issues in their communities. The guides are helpful as communities make decisions about how to handle specific problems, as well as to help citizens get "a feel for the game" of deliberation. Because democratic deliberation isn't the norm in collective learning and decision-making, organised deliberative forums with guides and moderators are an important way to introduce this approach and can serve communities well as they seek structured processes to take on challenging issues. We know that there is evidence that participating in formal face-to-face deliberation strengthens deliberative beliefs, skills, and habits; further, it is, as Burkhalter et al. (2002) argued, self-reinforcing. Challenged by the COVID-19 pandemic, there are many adaptations online that still foster the values of deliberation. The more people take part in deliberation, the more likely they are to be "motivated to deliberate when choosing among a range of modes of political communication" (ibid: 418).

Yet, one of the strengths of deliberative habits and practices is that their success does not *depend on* professionals, experts, or guides. As Lee and Mason-Imbody wrote in their 2013 article on everyday deliberation, "Too often, deliberation is misunderstood as a specialised technique or method. By examining everyday speech acts, we can show that deliberation is a natural part of talk—a native plant, not some exotic flower" (8).

While experts do play an important role in deliberative systems (Mansbridge et al. 2013: 13–17), they play a specific and limited role. There is a shortage of public space where everyday citizens are considered valuable and vital to naming, framing, and addressing public issues (Boyte 2009; Friedman and Rinehart 2017). The Citizens at the Center report, while focusing on the United States, made note of this, pointing out the lack or limited "opportunities for ordinary citizens to come together, deliberate, and take action collectively to address public problems or issues that citizens themselves define as important and in ways that citizens themselves decide are appropriate and/or needed" (Gibson 2006: 7). This is also evident in other parts of the world. Organisations like Freedom House, CIVICUS, and Amnesty International highlight the shrinking civic spaces in the face of rising authoritarianism worldwide, which in recent times has been further aggravated by the demands of the COVID-19 pandemic (Rupucci and Slipowitz 2021).

Thus, in our work we consider contexts where religious organisations develop and use deliberative guides for their work, as well as ways they use deliberation in everyday talk. As conceived in the literature, deliberation in everyday talk refers to deliberation that takes place outside formal contexts (e.g., forums) and instead over "backyard fences, during coffee breaks, and at the grocery store" (Mathews 2014: 80). We would add deliberation that occurs in various religious spaces such as in Bible studies, Mothers' and Fathers' Unions, at fellowship meals, guilds, associations and club meetings, and after worship.

1.5 The "Problem" of Religion

As noted in the introduction, there is a significant amount of writing that considers what is often understood as "the problem of religion" in deliberative democracy. We concur with the now widely accepted conclusion, particularly in the regions that are the focus of this volume, that religious reasoning should not be wholly excluded from public deliberation. It is beyond the scope of this book to engage the dizzying array of literature that takes up this issue, but we refer readers to the excellent discussion of this issue in "Religious

Reasons for Public Deliberation", in the *Oxford Handbook of Deliberative Democracy* (March and Stienmetz 2018). We would, however, highlight an important practical reason why religious reasoning should not be excluded from public deliberation. By religious reasoning, we mean that faith and religious standpoints serve as useful consideration and justification when deliberating on public issues. Around 60 percent of the world's population state that religion is important in their daily lives (Tamir, Connaughton, and Salazar 2021). In the United States, only 26 percent of the adult population say they are not religious (Newport 2017); in Zimbabwe, where our first case study is located, this number falls to 11 percent, and in Ghana, 5 percent (Crabtree 2010). While there are countries like Germany where more than 30 percent of the population identifies as agnostic or atheist and 57 percent of people report that religion does not occupy an important place in their lives (Tamir et al. 2021), this is the exception on a global level. Whether or not one accepts the liberal inclusivist argument that there are circumstances in which religious reasoning can play a legitimate role in democratic deliberation, the reality is that, in many if not most places in the world, when people deliberate, particularly on sensitive issues, the majority bring religious reasoning with them as demonstrated by the data above and in the places of focus in this book. They may not offer these religious reasons publicly, and they may couch them in secular terms that obfuscate their religious roots. Yet, they are present and this study names and acknowledges this.

We also expand the conversation about religion and deliberation beyond questions of the legitimacy of religious reasoning. There are a growing number of faith groups where democratic deliberation is incorporated into the life of the community as a religious practice (Neiheisel et al. 2009). Pastors are preaching about the ways that resources in their tradition—historical and scriptural—support democratic deliberation as an important path towards the more just, equal, and peaceful world that so many long for (Schade 2018). Churches and other faith communities are taking up difficult issues such as hunger, gender-based violence, and political polarisation. Everyday people are taking the risk to come together to face these challenges as a community, framing the issues in terms that make sense to them (rather than expert-led framings), naming what they hold most valuable, weighing difficult trade-offs in how to move forward, and identifying common ground in the midst of profound disagreement so that they can find ways to act together even when it is difficult, scary, and risky.

One example that highlights this work at the intersection of democratic deliberation and religious community is taking place in the Great Plains Conference of the United Methodist Church (UMC). The UMC is the second largest Protestant denomination in the United States, with more than 12 million members worldwide (Pew 2021). The church's *General Book of Discipline* outlines the structure and rules for the denomination as a whole. It includes language which prevents clergy from officiating same-sex weddings—and prevents ordination of gay, lesbian, transgender, and bisexual people who are open about and affirming of their identity, engaged in sexual activity, or partnered. The denomination has now split over these issues. The traditionalist branch became the Global Methodist Church (GMC) and is upholding restrictions on gay, lesbian, transgender, and bisexual clergy and same-sex marriages. The UMC is expected to reject the restrictions on gay, lesbian, bisexual, and transgender clergy and same-sex marriages at the upcoming 2024 General Conference. Individual churches and conferences have the option of remaining in the UMC or joining the new GMC.

In many churches, this has been and will continue to be a fraught and difficult issue where both clergy and congregants struggle with a path forward. It raises sensitive issues about scriptural interpretation, identity, family structure, ministerial authority, what it means to be a congregation and a denomination, and what it means to be a member of the Body of Christ. The question isn't only about what is right for the individuals in a specific congregation, but it is also about what role the church will play in the communities where they are located and what role the church will play in a rapidly changing world. What will the church be? What will it mean to be the church and be a part of the church in the midst of this?

The bishop of the Great Plains Conference of the UMC has recognised how fraught and intense these decisions will be. As the expected split between the UMC and the GMC drew closer, the Great Plains Conference decided to be proactive in embracing democratic deliberation as a way forward that might allow their churches to successfully navigate these challenges. Working with a range of clergy and lay leaders on all sides of the issue, the Great Plains Conference has developed a deliberation guide which names and frames the issue in terms that make sense to the people in churches, outlines options and potential actions, and articulates some of the trade-offs or drawbacks to the options and actions. The guide has three options so that the issue is not framed in binary terms but acknowledges the complexity of the issue at hand.

These deliberative guides have been and will be used in congregations across the conference. Moderators have been trained to facilitate deliberation that makes space for a range of voices and experiences. The deliberations are designed to help the churches make decisions and move forward in a way that honours the sincerely held religious beliefs and convictions of those within the church. The process is also intended to help congregants, individually and collectively, find ways to navigate the religious commitments at the heart of the churches' work. Many of these commitments, while religious, also have implications for well-being, justice, and equality both within the church and in the world where these churches are located. Approaching this issue deliberatively, rather than an adversarial or combative way, increases the possibility that a range of voices will be heard and considered, including voices that are often marginalised, and that a viable way forward will be identified.

The result may be that some congregations decide to break from the UMC and join the newly formed GMC. It may mean that some individuals realise that the decision that their congregation makes about how to move forward is not compatible with their theological commitments. It may be that some churches rethink central Christian categories such as hospitality and sin. We can imagine that many churches will develop initiatives that seek to address issues of welcome, inclusion, diversity, hospitality, and neighbourly love. But, in addition to whatever practical decisions are made, hundreds of people will have taken part in a democratic process of naming and framing an issue, deliberating about that issue, and identifying collective steps to take. In a time of intense polarisation and division, this is no small feat. It will have given hundreds of congregants the opportunity to get a "feel for the game", as Bourdieu puts it. When there are few culturally available models for non-combative disagreement and finding common ground across difference, the churches who are deliberating also serve a civic purpose by providing opportunities to practise listening, compromise, working together, and meaningful peace-making in the midst of polarisation and conflict.

1.6 Religious Organisations as Civic Nodes and Civic Gyms

There are some religious organisations and faith communities that do not value deliberative or democratic practices. Many faith groups will continue their political and public work with minimal attention to the importance of considering a range of voices, ideas, and experiences. For some faith groups, there is and will be little attention to how well they enable communities to have more of a say over their present or future. Aside from attending church and other religious gatherings because they are a place to worship, connect with and serve God, grow, and make the world a better place, some people are involved in faith groups because it is comfortable, a habit, and affirms their unearned power or privilege, and their control over others given that religious institutions tend to have hierarchical structures and power dynamics. The research in this volume will likely prove uninteresting, at best, to such religious institutions and people.

Yet, there are so many religious organisations and faith groups that are seeking a way forward where people can work together to address shared challenges, to cooperatively live out their theological commitments, and to understand each other better—but aren't sure how to do it in the midst of polarisation and deep structural problems that can seem overwhelming. A pastor from Texas, in the United States, noted,

> Lately it seems like people have lost their minds. My congregation has gone bat-shit crazy... I just want to find a way for us to be able to hear each other and talk to each other. To keep people around the table so we can figure things out together. But it is so volatile—people are so hurt and so angry, I am just not sure what to do.
>
> *Anonymous Mainline Protestant Pastor (2021)*

In another example, a Methodist pastor from Zimbabwe noted how important it was for the church to find a way to talk about gender-based violence among congregants. Before women were pastors, this was extremely challenging. But today, with women pastors, there is increasing space that allows for this much needed opportunity (Anonymous Methodist Pastor 2021). How can the church create spaces to address the challenges that all people face in their lives, including people who have been traditionally and historically marginalised and silenced?

In another mainline Protestant congregation in the United States, during "prayers of the people" on a Sunday morning in 2017, a middle-aged conservative woman prayed for then-President Donald Trump in a way that indicated her support of him and his presidency. Later, liberal members of the congregation, outraged by many of Trump's policies, approached the pastor and asked her what she was going to do about this. How could people like that be in our church? How could we pray for someone like that? In discussing this, the pastor noted how important it was to be able to be a church where everyone can attend, even people who see things very differently. This raises questions about how to be a church where congregants can hear each other and work together even in the midst of deep differences (Anonymous Pastor 2021).

And in Jacksonville, Florida, people who are without homes were sleeping on the steps of local churches. The homelessness rate across the United States varies, but in Florida it is nearly 5 percent of the population. Homelessness rates are even higher in cities like Jacksonville. Often, those without homes would set up all their possessions and create makeshift shelters directly outside the churches, even on the front steps. The churches, on the one hand, wanted to be welcoming and caring about their neighbours without homes. But they also struggled with issues of safety and comfort. What would the congregation think if there were people living on the steps of the church? What about the realities that come with wherever people live—food, waste, smells? What about the mental health challenges and addiction challenges these neighbours brought, literally, to the doors of the church (Kauffman 2021)?

These short examples highlight just a few contexts in which deliberation can be helpful: when there are questions that need answers and the answers are not clear, or when communities have problems to solve and look to everyday people in their congregations and communities to bring their experiences, wisdom, judgement, and energy to bear on these challenges. This approach is most helpful for those that are interested in better understanding the challenges and potential for faith groups as sites of democratic practice, and for those interested in experimenting with deliberative democratic practices that might be unfamiliar, risky, or challenging.

It may be that one or two individuals in a religious group are excited about deliberative democratic practices and find ways to introduce them in their religious communities. Or it may be that a leader in a church sees that the "old ways" of doing things are not working, and there is a need to experiment with new practices that might lead to more cooperation, more diversity, or different forms of ministry. There are many ways that deliberative democratic practices are introduced and take root in faith communities. The changes are rarely fast or easy. The research in this volume nonetheless highlights the finding that many find deliberative democratic practices to be enriching not only for the life of the church, but also that they contribute to strengthening partnerships and relationships in the community at large. We also find that there are variations and iterations of such practices in many cultures, even if they are not named as such. While there is a range of ways in which churches and faith communities can strengthen deliberative democratic practices, there are two models that have emerged in our research that are particularly helpful to explore. The first is the church or faith community that acts as a "civic gym" and the second understands the faith group as a node in a civic network.

In the first model, faith groups are a "civic gym" where people practise the work of community and cooperation, strengthening civic skills and muscles. In the gym, where they are "working out" with each other (or, getting a "feel for the game", as Bourdieu states), they figure out how to mobilise and connect with others, how to weigh options, how to balance acute needs with long term visioning, and how to talk to each other and make decisions together. Although she does not use the language of civic gym, Amy Erica Smith discusses this broader concept in her article, "Democratic Talk in Church: Religion and Political Socialisation in the Context of Urban Inequality", (2013) a case study of a municipal election campaign in a Brazilian city. She notes that "churches offer an important and often overlooked instance of civil society, one that is highly inclusive and provides frequent opportunities for interaction". She argues that this "political socialisation is especially important for educationally disadvantaged citizens and those living in low-education neighbourhoods, who may lack access to school-based civic education" (441). One important factor is that people are already going to church and already connecting with others about issues they care about. In the literature on deliberative democracy, a frequent lament of convenors who want to encourage deliberation is that it is hard to get people to show up. But people are already going to worship, taking part in small groups, Sunday school, and Bible studies. There is already a norm of meeting together to talk about things, often challenging and difficult things that people are struggling with.

Thinking of faith groups or churches as civic gyms does not diminish the other important roles that churches play—nurturing spiritual growth and fellowship, providing a context for communal worship and communion, and a place to carry out religious and spiritual callings. Rather, it names what is often already happening and provides an opportunity to build on it.

One example of this is St. John's Episcopal Cathedral in Jacksonville, Florida. For many years, retired pastor and member of St. John's, Reverend Gregg Kaufman, has been organising deliberative forums in the church. Internally, they have been deliberating over issues such as immigration, racism, end-of-life decisions, and the role of the church in a divided society. Kaufman believes that this practice in the civic gym, where congregants are able to engage with each other around complex, fraught issues, has prepared them for deeper engagement in their community. It has helped to normalise deliberative talk as an important political and religious practice, allowing citizen-congregants to think together about what they hold valuable and to weigh trade-offs together in a spirit of discernment. In this particular example, the civic gym prepared the church to be a "node" in a community network. In this second model, the faith group or church as an institution is interacting with other institutions in the community: the public schools, local non-profits, or the police, for instance. The focus is on the institution of the church and the role it can play in fostering deliberative democratic practices in their community and networks that ultimately help to address needs and solve problems.

St. John's had the opportunity to collaborate with others in their neighbourhood, known as the Cathedral District, to help with neighbourhood development plans. The Cathedral District is a 36-block, 118-acre area in downtown Jacksonville. There are five historic churches in the neighbourhood and many parking lots that are used by parishioners on Sundays. Early in the process of assessing what to do about some of the challenges of the Cathedral District, a local non-profit interested in neighbourhood development and revitalisation, Cathedral District Jax (CDJ), sought help in addressing what they thought was a clear problem: too much parking and not enough development. Yet, CDJ was open to naming and framing exercises with residents and church members from the district, and, through this, discovered more to discuss.

This is a pattern that many communities find: when people are given the opportunity to name and frame issues together, it often uncovers a deeper story. Led by Kauffman, a small group of representatives from several of the historic churches, a resident of the neighbourhood, and a person rehabilitating homes in the neighbourhood met. After a lot of back and forth, many hours of brainstorming, and gathering concerns, the team developed a guide that would be used in deliberations about the future of the district. Residents of the local condominiums and members of the five churches—Historic Mt. Zion African Methodist Episcopal (AME), First Methodist, First Presbyterian, Basilica of the Immaculate Conception, and St. John's Episcopal Cathedral—met for a series of forums to discuss the future of the Cathedral District. The final report from the deliberations included the following: "Forum outcomes revealed significant interest in relationship building among District stakeholders through community festivals, tours, collaborative church events, and possibly establishing a community association to complement CDJ, Inc. efforts". It turns out the problem wasn't too much parking per se, but that people longed for more green space, more trees, and more relationships among the various stakeholders. The CDJ board took the forum outcomes seriously. The first major initiative to come from the deliberations, Christmas in the Cathedral District, took place in 2019. There were lights, live music, a live nativity, a Bethlehem Marketplace, refreshments, shuttle transportation, and security. Several hundred volunteers and more than 1,000 visitors came to the district. Today, there are ongoing efforts not only to plant more trees and create a more walkable neighbourhood but also to find ways to address the challenges the community and citizens face due to lack of affordable housing, a shortage of living wage jobs, and addiction treatment.

In this example, we see that as members of the church developed their civic muscles through deliberation, they were able to become a node in the network in their community, strengthen cooperative relationships, welcome in a range of voices, and find common ground to address shared problems—even when there wasn't agreement on everything theologically or politically. This is a key feature of deliberative politics as many understand and practise it today. Unlike in Habermas' vision of deliberation, consensus is not the focus. The goal is not to get everyone to agree, but to find areas where people can act together and learn together in spite of disagreements that will remain.

1.7 Conclusion

Paul Feyerabend's 1975 *Against Method: Outline of an Anarchistic Theory of Knowledge* argued that there was nothing sacred, natural, or obvious about the scientific method. That essentially, we came to value knowledge validated by the scientific method for a range of historical, cultural, and social factors and not because this is the best way to arrive at helpful, valid, or trustworthy knowledge. One of the points he highlighted, both in writings and lectures more broadly, is that when we reify a particular method as *the* way to arrive at truth, we foreclose other meaningful and important ways of knowing. Feyerabend's insights are helpful in highlighting the importance of remaining open to different ways of knowing, learning, and understanding at the intersection of deliberative democracy and faith communities.

It is easy to get caught up in the idea that deliberation is something specialised that requires particular roles like a moderator and notetaker, or that it requires training programmes and funding. When people are overwhelmed with both the personal and political challenges inherent in living in a COVID-ravaged, late-stage capitalist global economy, it is easy to focus on small and manageable tasks like "how to frame an issue for deliberation" or "how many people came to the deliberation we sponsored after church on Sunday". Focus on method, on counting, on tracking, or reproducing "best practices" and "good programmes" often leaves out the creative learning that comes from everyday people working together to talk about, make sense of, and act together on their shared challenges (Frederickson 2003). Rigid methods do not leave room for productive failure or struggle, which often stifle the learning and change that are essential for citizens to collaboratively address problems. Additionally, this creativity and openness to productive failure and struggle is constitutive of many dynamic and growing faiths, including Christianity and African Traditional Religions, which we engage in this volume.

We wish to emphasise that we are not writing about a programme that religious groups should undertake or a method that people should learn. Rather, we are broadly interested in the big questions: How do we live well together? How can we solve problems together? How can institutions like the church play a greater role in sustainable development? These are answers we cannot know from reading, although reading can inform and enrich our journeys. These are also answers that cannot be determined by authority figures, although our leaders and guides can help challenge us and point us in productive directions. Science cannot give us all the answers about how to live together in healthy and moral ways and these are not answers we can arrive at by duplication of best practices or adherence to specific methods. The answers to the questions we are most concerned with in this book, and in our work as scholar-practitioners, are to be found in community: in the weeds, in the dirt, on the streets where we live and breathe and work, where we love and hurt and pray.

Ultimately, in this book we are making a case for learning together and acting together in the midst of the heartache and joy of the human experience. We provide ideas, steps, tips, theories, and guidance that we have found in our research, in our own communities and in communities that have been generous enough to allow us to walk alongside them as they have sought to find ways to live together that are better, more just, and more merciful. We do not argue that the path towards more peaceful, equal, thriving, and healthy communities is easy or assured. Yet, we explore the possibilities that lie between the tension of current challenges and the hope of transformation. Fundamental to our work is the hope in everyday people to struggle together, and to create positive change together. We do not believe that this is assured or that this is our fate, but that with hard work, care, attention, community, and effort, we can often make progress towards this.

In 1992, Václav Havel, political dissident and president of both the former Czechoslovakia and the Czech Republic, gave an address at University of Wrocław and spoke of the dissidents who

> despite the risks involved and the uncertainty of any real changes resulting, repeated over and over again that the emperor was wearing no clothes. This Sisyphean, almost quixotic stance originated mainly in the moral or existential field, in a heightened feeling of personal responsibility for the world. That is, the political activity of the dissidents had, far more obviously than it might have in conditions of freedom, a spiritual or moral dimension. Their way of thinking

and behaving, their values, the claims they made, their style of work, their standards of success and failure... can rightly appear inappropriate, alien, impractical, and idealistic when transferred to real politics in democratic conditions.

As we face a world that many perceive to be increasingly chaotic and perhaps irrecoverable, where our best hopes can seem silly and wildly unrealistic, it is helpful to be reminded that even in the most difficult times, there is the possibility that things might be otherwise. Although not *sufficient* for bringing about the world we long for, it is *essential* that there are people who continue work that can seem, in our current day and age, Sisyphean.

There is indeed an important "spiritual and moral dimension" to this belief in the possibility of a different world. The work of relationships, change, and growth is slow and often mundane, and it requires people to take a long, impractical view of shared life together that is unreasonably undeterred by election cycles and current events. The work is certainly long and hard, but the hope is that efforts such as those described in this volume will add to the possibility that things might be otherwise and encourage those who share similar commitments to continue, even when things seem inappropriate, alien, impractical, and idealistic.

References

Anonymous Mainline Protestant Pastor from Ohio, United States. (February 2019). Proceedings of the Kettering Foundation Research Exchange, "Faith-Based Organizations as Sites for Public Deliberation".

Anonymous Mainline Protestant Pastor from Texas, United States. (May 2020). Proceedings of the Kettering Foundation Research Exchange, "Faith-Based Organizations as Sites for Public Deliberation".

Anonymous Methodist Pastor from Harare, Zimbabwe. (2021). Interview by Kudakwashe Chitsike.

Bächtiger, André, Niemeyer, Simon, Neblo, Michael, Steenbergen, Marco, and Steiner, Jürg. (2010). "Disentangling Diversity in Deliberative Democracy: Competing Theories, Their Blind-Spots, and Complementarities", *Journal of Political Philosophy*, 18(1): 32–63. doi.org/10.1111/j.1467-9760.2009.00342.x

Barber, Benjamin. (1984). *Strong Democracy: Participatory Politics for a New Age*. Oakland, CA: University of California Press.

Bayat, Asef. (2012). *Life as Politics: How Ordinary People Change the Middle East* (2nd ed.). Stanford: Stanford University Press.

Bourdieu, Pierre. (1977). *Outline of a Theory of Practice*. Cambridge: Cambridge University Press.

Bourdieu, Pierre. (1990). *The Logic of Practice*. Stanford: Stanford University Press.

Boyte, Harry. (2005). *Everyday Politics: Reconnecting Citizens and Public Life*. Philadelphia, PA: University of Pennsylvania Press.

Boyte, Harry. (2009). *Civic Agency and the Cult of the Expert*. Dayton, OH: Kettering Foundation. Viewed from www.kettering.org/sites/default/files/product-downloads/Civic_Agency_Cult_Expert.pdf [Date accessed July 2, 2021].

Boyte, Harry, Elkin, Stephen, Levine, Peter, Mansbridge, Jane, Ostrom, Elinor, Sołtan, Karol, and Smith, Rogers. (2009). "Summer Institute of Civic Studies: Framing Statement." Viewed from http://activecitizen.tufts.edu/circle/summer-institute/summer-institute-of-civic-studies-framing-statement [Date accessed July 3, 2021].

Bretherton, Luke. (2016). *Resurrecting Democracy: Faith, Citizenship, and the Politics of a Common Life*. Cambridge: Cambridge University Press.

Burkhalter, Stephanie, Gastil, John, and Kelshaw, Todd. (2002). "A Conceptual Definition and Theoretical Model of Public Deliberation in Small Face-to-Face Groups", *Communication Theory*, 12 (4): 398–422. doi.org/10.1111/j.1468–2885.2002.tb00276.x.

Charmaz, Kathy. (2014). *Constructing Grounded Theory* (2nd ed.). Thousand Oaks, CA: Sage Publications.

Crabtree, Steve. (August 31, 2010). "Religiosity Highest in World's Poorest Nations", Gallup News. Viewed from https://news.gallup.com/poll/142727/religiosity-highest-world-poorest-nations.aspx [Date accessed July 1, 2021].

Feyerabend, Paul. (1975). *Against Method: Outline of an Anarchistic Theory of Knowledge*. Minneapolis, MN: University of Minnesota Press.

Frederickson, George. (2003). *Easy Innovation and the Iron Cage: Best Practice, Benchmarking, Ranking, and the Management of Organizational Creativity*. Dayton, OH: Kettering Foundation. Viewed from www.kettering.org/catalog/product/easy-innovation-and-iron-cage-best-practice-benchmarking-ranking-and-management [Date accessed October 2, 2021].

Friedman, Will and Rinehart, Chloe. (2017). "The Fix We're In: What Americans Have to Say about Opportunity, Inequality and the System They Feel Is Failing Them", A Public Agenda Learning Curve

Research Report. Viewed from www.publicagenda.org/files/TheFix
WereIn_PublicAgenda_2017.pdf [Date accessed June 29, 2021].

Gibson, Cynthia. (2006). *Citizens at the Center: A New Approach to Civic Engagement*. Washington, DC: Case Foundation. Viewed from http://casefoundation.org/wp-content/uploads/2014/11/CitizensAtTheCenter.pdf [Date accessed September 4, 2021].

Habermas, Jürgen. (1993). *Between Facts and Norms: Contributions to a Discourse Theory of Law and Democracy*. Cambridge, MA: MIT Press.

Havel, Václav. (December 21, 1992). Address at University of Wrocław. Viewed from http://old.hrad.cz/president/Havel/speeches/1992/2112_uk.html [Date accessed July 21, 2021].

Hennessy, Rosemary (ed). (1993). *Materialist Feminism and the Politics of Discourse*. New York: Routledge.

Kauffman, Gregg. (May 2021). Proceedings of the Kettering Foundation Research Exchange, "Faith-Based Organizations as Sites for Public Deliberation".

Lee, Amy, and Mason-Imbody, Erika. (2013). "Deliberative Opportunities in Everyday Political Talk", *Connections: The Annual Journal of the Kettering Foundation*, 8–11. Viewed from www.kettering.org/sites/default/files/periodicalarticle/Connections_2013_Lee_Imbody.pdf [Date accessed July 23, 2021].

Mansbridge, Jane, Bohman, James, Chambers, Simone, Christaino, Thomas et al. (2013). "A Systemic Approach to Deliberative Democracy", in James Parkinson and Jane Mansbridge (eds.), *Deliberative Systems: Deliberative Democracy at the Large Scale*. Cambridge: Cambridge University Press, 1–26.

March, Andrew and Steinmetz, Alicia. (2018). "Religious Reasons in Public Deliberation", in Andre Bächtiger, John Dryzek, Jane Mansbridge, and Mark Warren (eds.), *Oxford Handbook of Deliberative Democracy*. Oxford: Oxford University Press, 203–217.

Marion Young, Iris. (2002). *Inclusion and Democracy*. New York: Oxford University Press.

Mathews, David. (2014). *The Ecology of Democracy: Finding Ways to Have a Stronger Hand in Shaping Our Future*. Dayton, OH: Kettering Foundation Press.

Neiheisel, Jacob, Paul Djupe, and Sokhey, Anand. (2009). "Veni, Vidi, Disseri: Churches and the Promise of Democratic Deliberation", *American Politics Research*, 37(4): 614–643. doi.org/10.1177/1532673X08324216.

Newport, Frank. (2017). "2017 Update on Americans and Religion", Gallup News. Viewed from news.gallup.com/poll/224642/2017-update-americans-religion.aspx [Date accessed July 21, 2021].

Pew Research Center. (2021). "Religious Landscape Study". Viewed from www.pewforum.org/religious-landscape-study/ [Date accessed July 21, 2021].

Rupucci, Sarah, and Slipowitz, Amy. (2021). "Freedom in the World 2021: Democracy under Siege," Washington, DC: Freedom House. Viewed from https://freedomhouse.org/sites/default/files/2021-02/FIW2021_World_02252021_FINAL-web-upload.pdf [Date accessed January 20, 2022].

Schade, Leah. (2019). *Preaching in the Purple Zone: Ministry in the Red-Blue Divide*. Lanham, MD: Rowman & Littlefield.

Schüssler Fiorenza, Elisabeth. (2003). "Re-Visioning Christian Origins: In Memory of Her Revisited", in Kieran O'Mahony (ed.), *Christian Origins: Worship, Believe and Society*. London: Continuum International, 225–250.

Schüssler Fiorenza, Elisabeth. (2011). *Transforming Vision: Explorations in Feminist Theology*. Minneapolis, MN: Fortress Press.

Smith, Amy Erica. (2017). "Democratic Talk in Church: Religion and Political Socialization in the Context of Urban Inequality", *World Development*, 99: 441–451. doi.org/10.1016/j.worlddev.2017.05.032.

Tamir, Christine, Connaughton, Aidan and Salazar, Ariana Monique. (July 20, 2020). "The Global Divide", Washington, DC: Pew Research Center. Viewed from www.pewresearch.org/global/2020/07/20/the-global-god-divide/ [Date accessed August 2, 2021].

Townes, Emilie. (2006). *Womanist Ethics and the Cultural Production of Evil*. New York: Palgrave Macmillan.

United Nations High Commissioner on Refugees. (2021). Statistical Yearbooks. Viewed from www.unhcr.org/statistical-yearbooks.html [Date accessed November 10, 2021].

World Inequality Database. Viewed from https://wid.world [Date accessed September 11, 2021].

2
CASE STUDY 1: RELIGIOUS SPACES AND GENDER-BASED VIOLENCE

A Deliberative Approach to Voicing our Pain

2.1 Introduction

This chapter brings a gender lens to religion and deliberative democracy. Through a case study in Zimbabwe, we explore how religion can condone, allow, or validate violence, including political violence, targeted at women. A key feature of this phenomenon is the expected silence of women in many religious environments. While acknowledging the relative advancement of women in religion and politics in some contexts, in this research, the authors seek to surface atrocities against women in Zimbabwe's politics and the role of religious organisations in addressing the harm from such atrocities and in preventing future occurrences. The chapter draws on examples from African Traditional Religion (ATR) and Christianity, although the insights are intended to be helpful across traditions. Our research suggests that deliberative spaces in religious organisations, where women often form the largest part of the congregation, can be fertile ground for addressing societal issues such as violence against women.

Gender-based violence (GBV) is a global phenomenon that exists regardless of race, class, economic status, ethnic background, or religion. It is primarily perpetrated by men against women, children, transgender, and non-binary people. The Universal Declaration of Human Rights (UDHR) promotes the dignity and worth of the human person and the equal rights of men and women. In its preamble, it specifies sex as being among the impermissible grounds of differentiation and provides an equal protection clause in Article 7. Although the UDHR has no legal effect, it is morally binding. Provisions for equality in the enjoyment of rights are provided in all the major human rights covenants of the United Nations and are signed by its members. Equality is not only a fundamental right, but also recognised in SDG 5 as a necessary foundation for a peaceful, prosperous, and sustainable world.

Although described as GBV, this chapter focuses on violence against women as defined by the Declaration on the Elimination of Violence Against Women. Article 1 of the declaration describes violence against women as

> any act of gender-based violence that results in, or is likely to result in, physical, sexual or psychological harm or suffering to women, including threats of such acts, coercion or arbitrary deprivation of liberty, whether occurring in public or private life.
>
> *United Nations (1993)*

Violence against women is often regarded as a domestic issue because the perpetrators are often intimate partners of the victims. For this reason, there has often been the notion that it should be addressed in that private space. Yet, even when violence takes place in the home, it is still an issue of human rights and public concern. As we have noted previously, "the personal is political". That said, violence against women is not limited to just the private space but occurs in public places as well. In politics, as in the home, there is an always-present threat of violence to women—irrespective of class, relationship status, dress, race, or nationality. Because of this, women's voices are often muted by the fear of actual, threatened, or anticipated violence. This ever-present threat, whether explicit or subtle, shapes cultural and religious understandings of what it means to be a woman and shapes the lived experience of people who identify as women.

This chapter focuses particularly on sexual violence against women in the public space and the responses (or the lack thereof) of religious groups. With an insider's perspective, we examine this theme within the context of politics in Zimbabwe and its intersection with religion. We particularly focus on practices of ATR and Christianity. Given that women are the majority in most religious spaces, this chapter explores how women report sexual violence and seek redress in religious contexts which often claim to be spaces of support, care, and refuge for those experiencing harm. If women do not utilise such spaces, why not? How can such spaces better respond to violence against women? Religion plays a vital role in women's cultural lives and the church would seem to be an ideal setting for reporting and collectively addressing such atrocities.

Framing violence against women as a human rights violation implies an important global conceptual shift. It recognises that women are not exposed to violence by accident, or because of an inborn vulnerability. Instead, violence is the result of structural, deep-rooted discrimination which states and institutions have an obligation to address. Preventing and addressing violence against women is a legal and moral obligation. It requires legislative, administrative, and institutional measures and reforms. It also necessitates the eradication of gender stereotypes which condone or perpetuate violence against women and underpin the structural inequality of women.

The acceptance of violence against women as a human rights violation has led many countries to develop comprehensive legal frameworks and specific institutions and policies to promote women's rights and prevent violence against women. This, however, has not put an end to the scourge. Data released in 2021 by the World Health Organization indicate that globally, about one in three (30 percent) of women worldwide have been subjected to physical and/or sexual violence in their lifetime. Over a quarter of women aged 15–49 years who have been in a relationship have been subjected to physical and/or sexual violence by their intimate partner at least once in their lifetime. The collection of this data shows that there is growing awareness of the nature and impact of violence against women around the world, but the path to ending it is not yet clear. There are still obstacles to women's access to justice, resulting in widespread impunity for violent behaviour towards women. Considerable efforts are still required to promote women's and girls' autonomy, safety, and choice, and to ensure the realisation of the right of women and girls to a life free from violence and the threat of violence.

Our suggestion in this volume, which is in line with the existing literature on the topic, is that it will not be possible to prevent violence against women or eradicate stereotypes which condone and perpetuate it exclusively through changes to law, policy, or official church teachings. Rather, for true change to occur, everyday people need to be engaged in understanding and addressing these issues. While deliberation is not the only way this can happen, we argue that it is an important part of moving towards widespread change.

Gender equality and the emancipation of women are important factors for global economic, social, and democratic progress—and for the development of human society. Yet, religious institutions have often been accused of perpetuating inequality, either by their silence or their active participation in such inequality and violence (Nakashima Brock and Parker 2002; Oduyoye 2005). Social factors such as the treatment of women are influenced by religion and this can positively or negatively influence progress, equality, and freedom, depending on how a particular society interprets religious teaching. Here, we suggest that by centring the experiences of women and creating deliberative space in religious contexts for people, men, and women to engage this issue, religious groups—and institutions will be better equipped to reduce violence against women and improve the conditions which lead to this.

2.2 Violence against Women in Zimbabwe

Violence against women is a part of Zimbabwean society stemming from the patriarchal system where gender equality is not accepted even though it is officially enshrined in the constitution. In both traditional and religious culture, men and women are not equal, and women often remain under the guidance of the significant men in their lives: fathers, husbands, and brothers. According to the 2015 Zimbabwe Demographic Health Survey (ZDHS), 28 percent of women reported experiencing violence, and 27 percent of women aged 15–49 years reported that they had experienced sexual violence at least once at some point in their lives (Zimbabwe National Statistics Agency and ICF International 2015). The ZDHS does not collect data on politically motivated gender violence, but an independent study carried out by non-governmental organisations (Research and Advocacy Unit 2010) noted that 52 percent of the study sample stated that they had been victims of politically motivated violence. Rape was reported with a surprisingly high frequency: 2 percent reported being personally raped; 3 percent reported that a family member had been raped; and 16 percent reported that they knew someone in their community who had been raped (Research and Advocacy Unit 2010).

Patriarchy also manifests itself in the sphere of politics (Zimbabwe Human Rights NGO Forum, 2006). Women in politics are perceived as against cultural norms, as leadership roles are typically understood to be for men. When women participate in public life, their sexuality, marital status, body, dress, and competency come under intense scrutiny in ways that men are not subjected to; this is to discourage and demoralise them (Krook 2017). Violence against women often happens because the women are engaged in political activities, as supporters and candidates, or they are closely related to male political officials or electoral office candidates.

Zimbabwean women's stories about politically motivated violence over the last 40 years have been documented by local and international NGOs but never officially acknowledged or addressed by the government. Kudakwashe Chitsike, one of the co-authors of this book has had contact with Zimbabwean women over a period of more than 10 years through various networks. Where data is from interviews undertaken by Chitsike, the names and any identifying information of the interviewees are withheld at their request in order to protect their identity and safety.

Politically motivated sexual violence against women in Zimbabwe has been reported since the liberation war that took place between 1964 and 1979 (Manyonganise 2015). Rape is used to weaken and punish women during war and other political conflicts, limiting female participation as candidates or voters. Rape was documented during the Matabeleland massacres, known as Gukurahundi, in the 1980s (Catholic Commission for Justice and Peace in Zimbabwe and the Legal Resources Foundation 1997). A commission of inquiry was held to investigate, but it was never made public. In 1999, President Robert Mugabe (then-President of Zimbabwe) called this period a "moment of madness". In a 2015 interview, President Mugabe criticised the behaviour of the soldiers again, saying it was "very bad" but he put the blame on renegade soldiers. Women who were sexually assaulted during that period spoke openly about it, but with a lot of rage and pain (Interview 2020). Rape was also reported in the 2000 and 2002 elections. During the 2008 election period, it was widely reported by local and international organisations. Again, the government did not acknowledge it. Academic researchers and investigative journalists have been documenting rape as a Zimbabwe African National Union–Patriotic Front (ZANU–PF) political strategy (Hodzi 2012; Human Rights Watch 2019). Rape is used as a tool for repressing political opposition and winning elections.

During the 2008 election period, hundreds of women were subjected to sexual violence because of their political affiliation, or because their husbands or fathers were opposition activists (Research and Advocacy Unit and Zimbabwe Association of Doctors for Human Rights 2010). The main reasons these women were violated was to punish them and their families for supporting the opposition political party, the Movement for Democratic Change (MDC). Many of the women interviewed stated that while being raped, the perpetrators made it clear that they were intending to make an example of them: that in the absence of the male figure who was directly involved in politics, the women were being raped to show them and others the consequences of supporting the opposition. The police would not take reports of political violence, claiming that they had orders from their superiors not to accept such reports. Survivors interviewed stated that when they tried to report they were turned away once the police realised the matter was "political". They were told to go back home with promise of a follow up, which never happened, or they were threatened with arrest as they were accused of being the perpetrators.

A large number of the women reported what happened to their political party, and where the party could assist, they did so by ensuring that victims received the medical attention that they required, placing victims in safe houses, or assisting with burials when members were murdered as a result of the violence (the latter being done primarily for senior party members). Because the party was inundated with reports of violence across the country, they failed to provide help for everyone, especially women victims of sexual violence. The number of victims and violations will never be known, as some of the victims went to their graves with their stories of 2008 unspoken.

Many women kept their painful stories of rape to themselves for the reasons mentioned above; however, some women turned to civil society organisations that they knew and trusted, especially those identified as women's organisations. While these organisations attest to being inundated with reports of sexual violence, they were not fully equipped to offer shelter, clothing, food, medical, trauma counselling, or legal assistance. Very few women stated that they reported to their religious leaders because a sense of shame and self-blame inhibited them. The fact that these religious leaders were predominantly male also made the women hesitate. They didn't think they would receive the help they needed, especially after being turned away by the police. It is not surprising that the narratives of rape that occurred in 2008 and its consequences are still unfolding today; individual women have personal reasons for when they choose to speak out as doing so may have adverse consequences on their spouses, families, and communities.

Women suffered immensely as a result of politically motivated rape. Although many physical injuries have healed over time, many have permanent reminders—scars, post-traumatic stress disorder (PTSD), and other lingering medical conditions as a result of the sexual violence. Some women were infected with human immunodeficiency virus (HIV) and sexually transmitted infections (STIs); others became pregnant and gave birth to the children of their rapists, creating intergenerational trauma. As one interviewee noted:

> When my child asks who is his father, what will I tell him, when I myself don't know? Do I tell him the circumstances of his conception? He is my son, I don't want to lie to him but how do I tell him, he is a product of a violent rape?

Others were abandoned by their husbands who stated they could not live with a victim of rape. Because the culture often sees wives as belonging to their husbands, once a woman has been raped, many believe she brings shame to the family. The spousal abandonment led to a loss of social status for many women in their communities (Research and Advocacy Unit and Zimbabwe Association of Doctors for Human Rights 2010). Politically motivated rape continues to happen in part because women are not believed and/or are encouraged to be strong and bear the pain as though nothing can be done to put a stop to it.

2.3 Religious Perspectives on GBV

Christian Perspectives

One of the major obstacles to ending violence against women is within religious spaces, where the belief by many men and women is that a woman who doesn't submit to her husband opens herself to violence as her husband attempts to discipline her. It is often not even seen as violence, but a way to teach women how to respect and honour their husbands. The issue becomes problematic with the interpretation of religious texts like Ephesians 5:22–33 (NRSV) which has such phrases as,

> Wives, be subject to your husbands as you are to the Lord. For the husband is the head of the wife just as Christ is the head of the church, the body of which he is the Saviour. Just as the church is subject to Christ, so also wives ought to be, in everything, to their husbands

and "Each of you, however, should love his wife as himself, and a wife should respect her husband".

When verses and traditions like this one are taken to mean women in general are expected to respect and honour and obey *all* men, no matter what, because they are men, this can lead to violence, including in public spaces. Such verses and traditions are also highly problematic when they are interpreted to mean that women are to tolerate abusive, controlling, or harmful behaviour from their husbands or other men. Additionally, Biblical verses, such as Titus 2:4–5 (NRSV), which implores "young women to love their husbands, to love their children, to be self-controlled, chaste, good managers of the household, kind, being submissive to their husbands", and Proverbs 31:27 (NRSV) which lauds the "capable wife" who "looks well to the ways of her household, and does not eat the bread of idleness" are often quoted to show that a woman's place is in the home and that she should not be politically active. By taking on leadership roles, women are perceived to be interfering with the natural order as stated by the church, where women are often encouraged to be submissive and allow men to lead.

Zimbabwe is a predominately Christian nation where the main religious groupings are Protestant Christianity, Pentecostalism, and Catholicism, and in smaller numbers, Islam, Hinduism, and Judaism. There are also traditional African beliefs which are oftentimes practised together with Christianity, particularly in the Pentecostal and apostolic churches (Jeater 2016). ATR is exclusively practised by only 10 percent of the African population. ATR is based on beliefs that Africans had before colonisation and they are varied according to geography, ethnicity, and culture.

Religion is both a personal and institutional reality for most Zimbabweans from a very early age, including in school. It is not surprising that religious teaching and affiliation provide a significant context for many people when they are confronted with violence, either as perpetrators or as victims. Often, the more a society grapples with economic and social problems, the greater the reliance on religion (Crabtree 2010). This has an effect on the status of women, their efforts for promotion and protection of their rights and their advancement, their efforts to shape their communities, and their ability to support and care for themselves and their families. As the problems increase, there is often a sense of hopelessness and helplessness, and people often turn to the church and other religious groups for solutions to poverty, unemployment, ill health, and family dysfunction. Unfortunately, this is often exploited by those who interpret or wield the religious teachings for their own self-interested ends. Sometimes, such persons have themselves inherited problematic theologies that undermine women. This is not unique to Zimbabwe, but by interrogating this dynamic and investigating what everyday people can do to address this in Zimbabwe, we can better understand possibilities for change and transformation across nations, traditions, and cultures.

In Zimbabwe, as in many African contexts, the Word of God, conveyed through the pastors, leaders, and religious teachings, deeply influences the values and standard of what is understood to be right. The churches also provide direct support to their members, including counselling. This can be both positive and negative: positive in that the victim can access healing and find a sense of safety, but it can also be negative as the teaching may be misconstrued to condone abusive behaviour. When it comes to addressing GBV, the Reverend Dr. Marie Fortune and Rabbi Cindy Enger argue that the task for both religious and secular leadership is twofold: (1) to recognise that religious beliefs, texts, and teachings can serve both as roadblocks and as resources for victims of violence, and (2) to deepen our examination of religious texts and teachings and explore new interpretations so that we minimise the roadblocks and maximise the resources for women (Fortune and Enger 2005). No woman should ever be forced to choose between safety and her religious community or tradition. She should be able to access the resources of both community-based advocacy and shelter *and* faith-based support and counsel. For her to do so, she needs these two resources to work collaboratively so that they can provide consistent advocacy and support for victims and survivors and participate in the process of holding perpetrators accountable.

Phyills Trible (1984) points out that Christian Scriptures contain many stories of violence against women: for example, Dinah (Genesis 34), Tamar (2 Samuel 13), the Levite's concubine (Judges

19), Jephthah's daughter (Judges 11), Vashti (Esther 1), Suzannah (Daniel 13), and the persistent widow in Luke's Gospel (Luke 18). In addition to quietly lurking in the history and collective consciousness of the Christian tradition, these stories are used to normalise violence against women, not just by the perpetrators but also by many religious leaders to explain GBV in ways that do not advance a change in policy. Such "justification" is often echoed by the general public in everyday parlance. Additionally, verses such as 1 Peter 3:1–6 ("Wives, submit to your husbands...") and Ephesians 5:21–24 ("Wives, be subject to your husbands as to the Lord, for the husband is the head of the wife...") are frequently invoked in order to encourage women to accept and tolerate violence from their husbands. The blame is too often placed squarely on the woman, leaving her with nowhere to go to seek protection, recovery, help, and comfort.

It is important to note that proof-texting (using short/single verses from the Bible to justify a particular belief or doctrine) is often used to legitimise the subjugation of women, as mentioned above. When this is done, it is important to examine such readings in view of the entire passage, as well as refer to supporting text. Christian scriptures, often called the Old Testament and the New Testament, are a collection of texts written over centuries. The texts contain prayers, letters, law, poetry, and parables, to name only a few. While proof-texting is often used to support a particular view, it fails to reflect the complexity, vision, and mystery of Christian scripture. The context of a particular verse, the period it was written, who wrote it, where it was written, and what was happening around the author are essential to understanding the fullness of the text and how people today might use it to guide their actions.

There is a long tradition in Christian history, and in the Jewish tradition from which Christianity emerged, of discerning the meaning of texts in conversation with teachers and others in a religious community. While women have too often been left out of this process of interpreting texts, there is strong evidence that women had important roles in early Christian communities as believers grappled with what it meant to follow the teachings of Jesus and make sense of his life, death, and resurrection in the midst of struggle (King 2003; Schüssler Fiorenza 1983). For instance, Paul's letters highlight the tension that early Christian communities faced as they sought to live in faithful community, honouring a vision of justice and hope within the context of imperialism, political strife, and widespread inequality and injustice.

We argue here that in deliberating together about the meaning of texts that deal with gender and violence, and collectively grappling with the patriarchal interpretations that lead to the dismissal, abuse, rape, and killing of women, a path opens to understanding these authoritative texts in new and more just ways. Even given the fraught history of Biblical texts that have been used to harm, many theologians and everyday people use this same Bible as a starting place to imagine and build faith communities that protect women, support women, and honour women's role as leaders in the church and greater society.

One approach to this work has been to better understand and highlight the narratives of women in Biblical texts, who often played important roles as leaders, prophets, and disciples. One example is Deborah. She was a judge as well as a warrior, poet, prophet, singer, and songwriter. She was understood to be a wise and courageous woman. Deborah is one of the few women in the Hebrew Bible known for her own faith and actions without being attached to a man. Her story is told in the book of Judges. Other examples in the New Testament are Junia, who was named as an apostle (Romans 16:7), and Mary Magdalene, a follower of Jesus who was present at the crucifixion, the burial of Jesus, and chosen as the first follower of Jesus to encounter the risen Christ. In addition to highlighting women in the Bible who had positions of authority and leadership, another approach is to also cite relevant scriptures that can be read to support gender equality, inclusivity, and justice. One example is the baptismal formula in Galatians 3:28 which states that there is neither male nor female and that all are one in Christ.

These approaches can serve as important starting points for deliberation about the role of women in society and the church and, relatedly, appropriate Christian responses to abuse of and violence against women.

It is also necessary and important to frame violence against women as a sin, as it is the spiritual, physical, and psychological harming of another. Violence against women must be seen to be unacceptable, as it is inconsistent with many understandings of God as standing with the vulnerable and powerless, and speaks judgement against those who choose to assert their power in ways that are harmful to others (e.g., Luke 17:1–2). It is important to note that deliberation about a wicked problem does not preclude specifying boundaries of the conversation. An elder in one of the churches in Zimbabwe stated that anyone using the Bible to condone or perpetuate GBV doesn't understand the extent to which love should be understood to be at the centre of the Christian tradition. Some pastors in other churches deliberately preach misinterpretations to perpetuate the subjugation of women. He went on to say that "Anyone who has taken the time to study the Bible extensively will tell you that the essence of God is love and violence does not have a place where there is love" (Anonymous Elder Interview 2021).

In order to shift outdated and harmful views of women as subordinate and deserving of abuse, harm, and suffering, churches and religious leaders can create democratic and deliberative spaces for more deeply understanding the stories and traditions in Judaism and Christianity where women are powerful, respected, and protected from harm. It is essential that women's voices and experiences are central to making sense of religious texts and teachings, honouring the Christian tradition where texts are the starting point—but not the ending point—of a sound, just, and loving theology. Women should be encouraged to study the Bible with fresh eyes, where their own experiences and views are fundamental to making sense of what is fair, holy, sinful, and possible.

Religious groups are working more and more with secular civil society to fight GBV, especially after the enactment of the Domestic Violence Act in 2007. In a 2021 interview, a reverend in the Methodist church in Zimbabwe said that his church developed a gender and development policy with the assistance of organisations in the women's movement and the Zimbabwe Council of Churches. This policy has been published and disseminated within the church. The reverend acknowledged that the church's attempts to eliminate

GBV are hampered by patriarchal beliefs which have been embedded in religious teachings to continue to oppress women. He argues that this was never the intention of the teachings. The interrelationship between religion and culture cannot be understated as they influence society's attitudes towards women.

The Methodist church has a gender desk set up to assist anyone with any gender issues, including discrimination at the workplace, sexual harassment, and GBV. It was from this desk that the gender policy was crafted to ensure that the church is keeping abreast with gender developments locally and internationally, while recognising the church's role in providing for family and (in turn) community harmony. The aim of the desk and the policy is to ensure that when a person is reporting something traumatic, they should feel comfortable to open up, knowing that the matter is being handled by a person who has the necessary expertise and will not trivialise it. When cases of GBV are reported, the desk provides a referral pathway to medical facilities and reporting to the police. In cases of domestic violence, it can be a space to bring in the perpetrator and the victim together to find out where the problems lie and through counselling find a way to resolve the issues without resorting to violence. Such desks are one example of how churches in Zimbabwe are challenging habits and behaviour related to GBV by listening to women and their experiences, and deliberating together about a way forward (Musodza et al. 2015). This would not be possible without openness to the experiences of women, the voices of women themselves, and willingness to both talk and act differently with respect to GBV in the church. Such desks will go a long way to bring the correct information on GBV to women who have concerns, and they will be a step towards addressing such issues without blaming or stigmatising women. The desks, however, should not be seen to benefit only women; they are attempting to bring about social change in communities.

As another example, the Catholic Church in Zimbabwe is seeking to empower women through self-help initiatives to end GBV. A diocese in the Masvingo province, through its humanitarian and development arm, Caritas, has started an initiative called Start, Awareness, Support and Action (SASA) Faith in Action. It aims to encourage peace and tranquillity (Kugwa 2021). Although led by the Catholic Church, several other denominations are also taking part, including Zion Christian Church, Reformed Church in Zimbabwe, and Full Gospel. Along with efforts to support women economically, an important aspect of the programme involves dialogue and deliberation efforts not only between couples but also religious leaders, local leaders, lay leaders, and SASA's leadership team. The purpose of ensuring that these processes include multi-stakeholders is to ensure that everyone knows their rights and what steps to follow should one be faced with GBV, either as a victim or a community or religious leader. These deliberative efforts in communities allow different voices to be heard, thereby promoting healthy conversations. The hope is that by the church taking a vocal role in destigmatising GBV, it will create a domino effect in the community, positively impacting individuals, households, business, organisations, and other faith and non-profit organisations.

Perspectives from ATRs

According to a Harvard professor, Jacob Olupona, the word "religion" is often problematic for Africans because it suggests that religion is separate from the other aspects of one's culture, society, or environment (Olupona 2015). Olupona notes that many Africans believe that religion is a way of life and can never be separated from the public sphere. Religion informs everything in traditional African society, including politics, art, marriage, health, diet, dress, economics, and death. Olupona goes on to emphasise that this is not to say that indigenous African spirituality represents a form of theocracy or religious totalitarianism, but rather many African spiritualities simply acknowledge that beliefs and practices touch on and inform every facet of human life. Therefore, African religion cannot be separated from the everyday or mundane, in the ways that this is sometimes conceptualised in the academic study of religion, or in certain European or US contexts where religion is often understood to be discrete and separable from the realm of the secular.

According to Prosper Muzambi, a leading thinker on ATR, in the traditional African beliefs there is a widespread belief in the spirits of ancestors. These are called *vadzimu* in Shona, the main indigenous language in Zimbabwe, and *amadlozi* in Ndebele, the second most common language in Zimbabwe (and also used in South Africa); deceased chiefs are called *mhondoro* in Shona. These ancestors continue to exist in the community, influencing and affecting life. They are believed to care for their descendants and share their experiences, though the living eye cannot see them. Communication with these ancestral spirits is usually achieved through mediums, *n'anga* (often called "witch doctors" in English), and powerful members of the community. It is believed that many events in life occur because of the spirit world; some people may believe that spiteful spirits known as *ngozi* are the cause of bad luck, illness, or death. They may even call upon these spirits for punishment or vengeance. Missionary Christianity undermined the value of *ngozi*, as people were made to think that they were a form of evil spirits and not a bridge towards peace. The co-existence of Christianity and ATR continues today, as many Zimbabweans believe that the current political situation continues because the wounds of the past have not been adequately dealt with. Although it is difficult to agree on timelines, these wounds include the liberation struggle, and the violence marking all general elections in Zimbabwe since 2000, in particular (Muzambi 2018).

By not addressing the past and continuing on this path, the wounds increase and fester, and the cycle is not broken: peace and harmony will never be achieved. Yet, so many value and desire peace and harmony. ATR's teachings related to the importance of addressing wounds of the past resonate with important parts of deliberative democratic theory that Noëlle McAfee outlines in her book, *Democracy and the Political Unconscious*. In the description of her book, she notes that when people are denied participation in shaping their own world, "whether through trauma or terror", a political unconscious arises that is characterised by "an effect of desires unarticulated, failures to sublimate, voices kept silent, and repression reenacted". She further highlights that "unless troubles are worked through, a political community risks continual repetition and self-destruction" (2008). Keeping in mind the importance of honouring the spirits of ancestors and the wounds of the past that have not been dealt with, we can see how deliberative democracy may have resonances with ATR where there is an emphasis on addressing and taking seriously what has been suppressed or ignored. The interplay between deliberative democracy and ATR can move towards addressing wounds of the past and honouring sacred and long-held beliefs that were violently suppressed by colonisers.

Zimbabwean politics is often characterised by violence, and there are different ways to deal with this. Traditional ways of fostering peace and understanding can be used together with deliberative democracy to address the ways people have been denied participation in shaping their world and have been held back by wounds of the past that remain unaddressed. By honouring ancestors and spirits, and by taking seriously the role that they play in the religious and daily life of Zimbabweans, there is the possibility to work through troubles and break the cycles of repetition and destruction that have been so often characterised by violence and loss. In both deliberative democracy and ATR, there is an important element of excavation.

Despite the negative elements associated with *ngozi*, their devastating effect can serve as a deterrent to violence before, during, and after elections. In interviews with survivors of sexual violence, many spoke about the unexplainable illnesses and deaths of perpetrators of political violence in their communities and they attribute this to *ngozi*:

> You cannot go on a killing and raping spree in the name of a political party and expect to continue your life as normal: the spirits of the departed and their ancestors are not at peace and will seek vengeance.
>
> *Anonymous Interview (2020)*

The majority of interviewees strongly believe in the *ngozi* yet they identify as Christians and are active members of their churches. In the same way that Christian teachings and ATR co-exist in a complex relationship in people's lives and spirits, ATR can also co-exist with democratic practices, where space is created to unearth what lies below, what has been repressed, and what is unsaid and unseen.

Although there are many differences between Christianity and the ATR, there are also similarities: they both recognise an omnipresent creator that oversees all living beings, they believe in good and bad spirits, and they value peace, truth, and justice (Idang 2015).

In approaching these questions from the perspective of democratic deliberation, we can explore perspectives and possibilities for addressing GBV that are grounded in religious conviction and practice. There is a small percentage of people in Zimbabwe that solely practise ATR; many people formally identify as Christian but often practise their African Traditional Beliefs together with Christianity. A Catholic priest stated that, essentially, African Traditional Beliefs are a part of all churches in Africa, as Christianity was brought to Africa and assimilated into the way of life, and continues to evolve even today.

> The way we worship and fellowship in Africa is very different from Europe or America: part of the differences are influenced by our cultures as Africans even though we are using the same Bible. We cannot run away from our traditional beliefs as this is who we inherently are.
> *Anonymous Catholic Priest Interview (2021)*

The ability to hold ATR and Christianity together speaks to a strength of the faithful, where believers may honour those who have gone before them, honour what works in Christianity, and recognise the parts of each tradition that no longer work for their context. This shows that there is room to grow and change and rethink the way things have always been done, explore that which has been silenced and repressed, and move forward in ways that bring together the old and the new in creative and meaningful ways. In the next section, we explore how deliberative and democratic ways of being might be fostered in the context of the vibrant religious life of Zimbabwe in order to address GBV.

2.4 GBV and Deliberative Conversations

A central focus of deliberative democracy is to bring people together to have a conversation about an issue that is of concern to them with the aim of weighing options that might help to address the problem. Deliberating on GBV will therefore involve a process that enables multiple viewpoints on what GBV means to various people while considering ways of addressing the problem. In addition to finding solutions, which is often not easy, the process should help to broaden understanding and opinions on the issues at hand.

Over the decades, as gender issues surfaced globally—particularly with the Convention on the Elimination of All Forms of Discrimination Against Women (CEDAW) and the post-Beijing Conference period following the declaration—conversations focused mainly on awareness creation, campaigning, and legal and regulatory frameworks. While these approaches were critical in highlighting the plight of the millions of women who suffered one form of violence or the other in their homes, communities, and places of work, in some ways, they limited the conversations to gender activists, researchers, feminists, and local and international organisations who either provide support to affected persons or helped to surface the issue of GBV. These mechanisms have been useful to a great extent, but they may also have alienated various segments of society who need to be part of the solution to GBV.

In this chapter we have focused on Christian groups, particularly in Africa, with references to African Traditional practices as these two interact. As demonstrated above, there are sacred texts and scriptures that have been interpreted in ways that justify violence against women in particular. Religious groups ought also to be in conversation with activists around the issues. In recent times, more efforts have been made to initiate gender programmes that go beyond accusing men of being the root causes of GBV and instead target men's participation in the solutions—for example, networks such as MenEngage (https://menengage.org). In addition to misinterpretations in religious and cultural practices, it is not unusual to hear commentary from both men and women suggesting that efforts in gender advocacy are Western constructs designed to destroy Indigenous cultures. Among other reasons, which are deeply seated in the destructive force of colonialism, such utterances are also because the issue of GBV is often not framed in ways that resonate with the majority.

Two key points are worth reiterating here. First, GBV is a human rights issue as discussed above. We do not seek to diminish this. The manner in which women are viewed in society influences the way they are treated. Violence and harmful cultural practices have a negative impact on women's rights in defiance of laws. In Zimbabwe, as in other parts of Africa and the world, the patriarchal and misogynistic attitude towards women in politics results in a skewed leadership scale unfavourable to women, who make up more than half of the world's population. Patriarchy sees women as incapable of handling power and responsibility in any leadership position, but more so in politics (Krook 2017). It portrays women as weak and refuses to acknowledge that women can make decisions that are binding for a society. These attitudes have emboldened perpetrators of violence against women. This attitude is by no means justifiable by the framing of the gender debate. Second, GBV is not a straightforward issue with easy answers; it is a wicked problem (Brown et al. 2010). Within the twin concepts of religion and culture, we recognise that GBV borders on the private and the public, faith and secular ideas, rationalisation, and normative practices.

It is with these complexities that we propose deliberative practices as a way of engaging GBV, as it provides the space for the multiple viewpoints, including looking at the issue from a gender dimension, and drawing in the voices of the victims, who are mostly women, as well as the voices of the perpetrators and other traditionally excluded groups.

The key assumption in deliberative conversation is that people are likely to come to the conversation if the issue is framed in ways that resonate with them. In other words, they must see some self-interest. This is distinct from "selfishness". At the other end of the spectrum, while altruism might seem laudable, it does not always compel people to act. Arguably, even altruism is a choice, often a choice in the choice-maker's interest. If we want people to contribute to solving problems, we must start from how the problems affect them, or impacts their lives and their life choices. These are not always obvious unless it is drawn out in words or in language that hits home. Here is an iteration of conversations co-author Ruby Quantson Davis has had on GBV, either in training workshops or in evaluating projects.

DAVIS: What will you do if your daughter comes home with black eyes, broken jaw and teeth, and says her husband beat her?
MAN: I will deal with that man! Possibly go beat him up or hire people to "rough him up".

It is notable that, in some instances, this question has been directed at men who worked in religious organisations or who are themselves clergy and/or are deeply rooted in patriarchal practices. They are not bad people; they are fathers who care about their daughters as they should. Their response should not attract judgement.

When they regain their composure from the shock of the question, they quickly retreat to traditional cultural approaches with responses like, "Well, we will sit as elders and discuss the issue and work towards reconciliation."

These responses demonstrate the tension in the instinctive reaction and the pull of cultural practices. Unless the issue of women's rights is framed in ways that invite these tensions into the conversation space, we lose an opportunity to search for solutions together and in ways that co-create new ways of understanding human rights and cultural traditions.

The framing of the issue could be situated within the very culture that people hold valuable, using metaphors, symbols, and personalities they value. In Zimbabwe, a revered and strong female figure, Mbuya Nehanda, was instrumental in the fight against colonialism. The same reverence is extended to Yaa Asantewaa, Queen Mother of Ejisu in the then-Ashanti Empire, now part of modern-day Ghana, who fought the British Empire in the famous War of the Golden Stool.

It is not unusual to hear men observe that they would like their daughters to be as brave and courageous as the heroines mentioned above. We have often presented gender issues through framing that invites people to consider the kind of woman they would like to raise in their daughters. In our own work in gender advocacy, community engagement, peacebuilding, and conflict resolution, we have had humbling moments when participants have observed they would like to raise daughters like us.

Deliberative spaces could help to accommodate the tensions people hold on such a culturally demanding issue as violence against women. Deliberative conversations provide ways of framing the issue in ways that capture what people hold valuable. These often revolve around issues of security, particularly the well-being of individuals and their relations as well as their self-preservation as seen in the conversation cited above. To ignore these is to make people feel vulnerable. Deliberation also opens the conversation by providing options towards finding solutions. It removes "them and us" and elevates the issue above binaries. It provides space for people to wrestle with their tensions. Most importantly, it provides a space where they are able to do this with others who care about the issue. The resulting outcomes are usually realised collectively: an approach that advances the potential for action. Can religious spaces that often attract a signficant percentage of the population provide deliberative spaces for various perspectives to engage on GBV?

2.5 Women's Voices in Religion and Politics

In interviews with African Christian religious leaders on the coexistence of religion and politics, we heard insightful responses around leadership and gender in the church.

One church leader observed:

> If a person decides to run for office, they must relinquish any post that they hold in the church, as their focus will be divided. We do not stop anyone from running for office; the

individual must make the choice. If that choice is politics the church accepts that and they will not be treated any different from any other church member. This is the position regardless of whether that person is a man or woman.

Anonymous Interview (2021)

Another church leader stated about his church,

> Our mission is to evangelise, not engage in politics. It is anyone's right to take up any position they want to. It is not that the church doctrines state that men or women should not engage in politics or take up leadership roles, but there is a misinterpretation of these doctrines.
>
> *Anonymous Interview (2021)*

From the responses, the church appeared "gender blind" regarding views on politics and religion. While on the surface, this sounded like there were equal opportunities for men and women, it was a disturbing posture, as it demonstrated a level of ambivalence to the gender disparities in political participation, sometimes occasioned and justified by scriptures.

First, it is important to highlight that for many people, politics is understood as partisan politics, associated with divisions and zero-sum games. If politics is conceived as a choice-making and decision-making in all aspects of life, it might generate a different conversation—one that recognises that women are making decisions and acting in various capacities and in various spaces in and outside the church. Our argument, therefore, is that the limited conceptualisation of politics coupled with gender roles often endorsed by religious practices makes the church unreceptive to women who have suffered violence.

Can the Church Be a Place of Refuge for Victims and Survivors of GBV?

In our work, we have learned that while the church can be a space for victims of GBV, there is an element of self-censorship based on what the victims think the reaction of the church will be. Victim blaming, even if not verbalised, is prevalent both in the church and the larger community. A thought expressed by one of the religious leaders is instructive:

> The church should be a place of solace and comfort but there are instances where it can also be a place of judgement. However, let's remember that the guiding principle of church and religious spaces is love above all else.
>
> *Anonymous Interview (2021)*

With regard to politically motivated sexual violence against women, some leaders acknowledged that it happens particularly during conflict, including elections, but they had no direct experience in their churches of this. The nature of the violence feels very personal. Many of the women documented reported that it is not an easy thing to talk about sex under any circumstances. It therefore is not surprising that many church leaders may not have direct experience with politically motivated sexual violence. The church leaders interviewed for this study were men, and they stated that there is space for women to talk amongst themselves about such sensitive issues and find ways to help each other.

Even though political violence in Zimbabwe has been reported for more than a decade, none of the women interviewed stated that they sought help at a church or with their religious leaders; rather, they went to women's organisations or to their political party. Churches in the communities where the violence was perpetrated were often regarded as being complicit, as people who sought refuge there were often told not to speak up or were further assaulted. The compartmentalism of politics and religion is part of the problem. Perpetrators are able to separate their political lives from their religious lives, and are therefore able to do terrible things in the name of politics and still view themselves as church folk. Robert Mugabe was a devout Catholic but was allegedly responsible for extreme violence when his political power was threatened. For example, the Gukurahundi genocide in the 1980s and the campaigns of violence during election periods between 2000 and 2008, amidst reports of murder and rape occurred during his presidency.

For the church to be seen to be a safe space for women, there is a need to be open about the reasons why women do not feel comfortable speaking up. The fact that some churches are having honest discussions about gender and women's rights is a step in the right direction, especially if these discussions are being facilitated by trained moderators. This could be an opportunity to use the deliberative approach, as it allows for honest discussions that bring in different points of view and weigh the pros and cons of any suggestions brought forward. One of the church leaders interviewed in 2021 stated that his church has female pastors that are keen to raise issues specific to women in the church. The value of speaking to someone who looks like you, or who has experienced the same challenges as you, goes a long way. This is not to say that the men are incapable of being sensitive about such issues. It is important for church spaces to discuss politics and the consequences for women—without making it only a women's issue—as this doesn't bring balanced solutions. Any violence in a community is the community's issue—not that of a particular gender, ethnicity, or other group of people.

There is room for the church to work with the state to create peace, justice, and strong institutions, as articulated in SDG 16, which recognises that conflict, insecurity, weak institutions, and limited access to justice remains a threat to sustainable development. This could be done by opening a space for deliberation between church and political leaders. In most African contexts, while the church may have the capacity to bring people together across differences to discuss peace and justice, this is challenging when the state is implicated in atrocities. In the Zimbabwean scenario, the state was allegedly responsible for the politically motivated violence against women. Because it works to its advantage, it will pay lip service to any attempts to work with the church—but there is no true collaboration to address the issue of violence against women. During politically tense periods, church groups have tried to engage with the government, but these attempts were met with disdain, and the churches were categorically told that they had overstepped. For example, in August 2020, Catholic bishops issued a pastoral letter accusing the government of human rights abuses and thwarting dissent when the police arrested citizens participating in an outlawed planned demonstration. The government issued a press statement against the pastoral letter which appeared in the news on 16 August 2020, in online media such as Al Jazeera and Reuters, calling it an "evil message" meant to stoke a "Rwanda-type genocide".

SDG 17 states that successful development can only happen with inclusive partnerships, with shared vision, and shared goals. The church must be seen to be one of these partners and both lay and ordained leaders in the church can find ways to work towards this ideal. The churches in Zimbabwe are considered civil society, working under the banner of faith-based organisations. These groups include the Zimbabwe Council of Churches, Zimbabwe Heads of Christian Denominations, and the Evangelical Fellowship of Zimbabwe. They partner with non- governmental organisations (NGOs) particularly on social and governance issues, where gender and politically motivated violence sit.

The church should be seen as a place for refuge during difficult times, not just for its congregants but for anyone requiring it. Yet, it is important to note that the priests or pastors are individuals who have their own political beliefs as well as their own fears and prejudices. They cannot handle it alone—it will take many everyday people who make up the church to make change possible. In spite of the general silence on this matter in the church, it was gratifying to hear one religious leader observe,

> In 2008, everyone was gripped with fear as political violence rocked the country. Women came to my parish, giving horrific accounts of gang rape. Some of them were raped by members of the same community. I was afraid but I did the best that I could under the circumstances.
>
> *Anonymous Interview (2021)*

There are those in the church trying to safeguard women, yet it will take more than just individuals acting alone. Theological education is required to change the problematic theology that perpetuates GBV, this in turn can change social perceptions. It cannot happen overnight, but when there are collaborative and deliberative efforts to raise awareness of gender inequality and sin of violence against women, efforts at emphasising the equality of men and women before God, and progress towards balancing the power dynamics, there is hope that someday the church may be a place of refuge for victims and survivors of GBV.

2.6 Do Women in Religious Spaces Have Agency?

Agency can be defined as the capacity to make individual and independent choices. According to feminist theorist Lois McNay, agency is "the capacity for autonomous action in the face of often overwhelming cultural sanctions and structural inequalities" (2000: 10). These are not typically words that describe women, even more so religious women, as they are so often socialised to abide by the rules that state that men are more inclined to leadership, activity, and a strong work ethic, whereas women are naturally nurturing, passive, and receptive. However, Saba Mahmood argues that much of feminist scholarship is based on Western standards and it is necessary to look at the cultural and historical background since "the meaning and sense of agency cannot be fixed in advance, but must emerge through an analysis of the particular concepts that enable specific modes of being, responsibility, and effectivity" (Mahmood 2004: 42).

Agency can manifest in different ways. According to Burke (2012), it can be

- resistant—resisting the status quo;
- empowering—changing the response to beliefs or practices in a positive manner;
- instrumental—focusing on the non-religious outcomes of religious practice; and
- compliant—bringing about change by conforming to the rules.

One example where women's agency has worked in traditional religions is the acceptance of female pastors in the Methodist church

(Marumo 2016). The different types of agency do not have to be mutually exclusive—they can be fluid depending on the situation, keeping in mind that change doesn't happen without tension. These ways of exercising agency are not foolproof. It is important to weigh the limitations that each approach presents, as enacting agency may result in ostracisation from the space that one is attempting to change.

Women must have accessible paths to exercise their agency if they believe that GBV should be addressed in the church. However, exercising agency in any space is influenced by factors such as residence, culture, education, and age, and can be challenging. Women, as the majority in most congregations, can use their groups and roles in the church to combat GBV, but they have to be prepared to encounter the "big man" syndrome, which looks at women's issues as trivial and that violence against them is their cross to bear. These women's groups are also not homogenous, as there are women who do not believe in equality and in female leadership. Violence against women is sometimes perpetuated by other women, reinforcing the cultural beliefs that men should lead and that men and women were created to fulfil different and complementary roles that tend to privilege the status of men (Burke 2014). Naming and framing the issue of GBV in a faith context creates the space needed to begin to identify a way forward. Rather than "yes" or "no" or "good" or "bad", naming and framing and the deliberation that follows provides a range of paths forward, and a range of actions to consider. The challenges of this work—and there are many—should not discourage women from bringing issues that are detrimental to them to church as they work for change. Violence in public places is not only a problem for women. It is a societal problem that requires a holistic solution.

The protection of women in religious spaces is, of course, contentious. Fundamentalist groups argue that controls and measures in place are there to protect women, and more liberal voices say these measures are oppressive as they foster discrimination, violence, and gender inequality. A deliberative approach presents an opportunity to facilitate equal voices for women, building on their agency in whatever form makes sense for them in their particular context, by increasing the extent to which their voices are heard and considered, and by encouraging full participation (Karpowitz et al. 2012).

2.7 Opportunities for Deliberation

There is room in religious spaces to address violence against women using democratic deliberative approaches, including giving space to the perspectives of victims, perpetrators, and those who perpetuate the systems that both allow and cause such violence. The framing of the conversations is critical. This framing needs to be inclusive to enable those that have traditionally been excluded to feel welcome and comfortable enough to participate. Election violence, as is common in Zimbabwe, is a community issue as it targets not only people who are actively involved in politics but also those who go out and vote, and even bystanders. It is a broader symptom of a lack of tolerance, peace, and unity triggered by a protracted lack of basic human needs being met, poverty, and unhealthy politics, among other factors. Peace, love for the other, and co-existence are all attributes that the church, and many other religious groups preach and have a responsibility to promote with actions rather than only words.

Women who were caught up in the violence need the space to talk about what they went through and collaborate across differences with others to address the root causes of the problem. Particularly because the majority of the congregants are women, the church should provide space for deliberation. From our fieldwork and research, we have hope that through deliberative democratic practices, the church *can* be a space where justice and accountability are strengthened and grow, ensuring that the systems that allow and promote such violence, along with the perpetrators who carry it out, can be held to account and reformed such that in the next election cycle GBV does not play a role. Each church and denomination will find a unique path to address these challenges, but counselling and support for the victims, perpetrators, and their families, to enable them to recover from the life altering events, is essential. Deliberative spaces form an important part of the process to meet the needs of individuals and communities who have already experienced GBV, as well as an essential role in creating opportunities for a shared understanding of GBV and the options to address it. Having such spaces will increase the chances of meaningful and successful collective action and peaceful co-existence in communities as intended by the SDGs.

References

Anonymous Sexual Violence Survivors documented between 2010–2020. Interviews by Kudakwashe Chitsike. Harare: Zimbabwe.

Anonymous Elder Interview. (2021). Interview by Kudakwashe Chitsike. Harare: Zimbabwe.

Anonymous Catholic Priest Interview. (2021). Interview by Kudakwashe Chitsike. Harare: Zimbabwe.

Anonymous Methodist Reverend Interview. (2021). Interview by Kudakwashe Chitsike. Harare: Zimbabwe.

Brown, Valerie, Harris, John, and Russell, Jacqueline (eds.). (2010). *Tackling Wicked Problems Through the Transdisciplinary Imagination*. New York: Routledge.

Burke, Kelsy. (2012). "Women's Agency in Gender-Traditional Religions: A Review of Four Approaches", *Sociology Compass*, 6 (2): 122–133. https://digitalcommons.unl.edu/cgi/viewcontent.cgi?article=1719&context=sociologyfacpub.

Burke, Róisín Sarah. (2014). *Sexual Exploitation and Abuse by UN Military Contingents: Moving Beyond the Current Status Quo and Responsibility under International Law*. Leiden, Netherlands: Brill. doi.org/10.1163/9789004208483.

Catholic Bishops Accuse Zimbabwe Gov't of Rights Abuses (August 16, 2020). *Al Jazeera*. Viewed from https://www.aljazeera.com/news/2020/8/16/cat

Catholic Commission for Justice and Peace in Zimbabwe and the Legal Resources Foundation. (1997). *Breaking the Silence, Building True Peace: A Report on the Disturbances in Matabeleland and the Midlands, 1980–1988*. Viewed from http://archive.kubatana.net/docs/hr/ccjp_lrf_breaking_silence_9904.pdf [Date accessed April 20, 2021].

Chiorazzi, Anthony. (October 6, 2015). "The Spirituality of Africa", *The Harvard Gazette*. Viewed from https://news.harvard.edu/gazette/story/2015/10/the-spirituality-of-africa/ [Date accessed October 20, 2021].

Crabtree, Steve. (August 31, 2010). "Religiosity Highest in World's Poorest Nations", Gallup. Viewed from https://news.gallup.com/poll/142727/religiosity-highest-world-poorest-nations.aspx [Date accessed December 1, 2021].

Fortune, Marie and Enger, Cindy. (March 2005). "Violence Against Women and the Role of Religion", Applied Research Forum, National Online Resource Center on Violence Against Women. Viewed from https://vawnet.org/sites/default/files/materials/files/2016-09/AR_VAWReligion_0.pdf [Date accessed November 9, 2021].

Hodzi, Obert. (2012). "Sexual Violence as Political Strategy in Zimbabwe: Transitional Justice Blind Spot?" Oxford Transitional Justice Research Working Paper Series: Debates. https://www.law.ox.ac.uk/sites/files/oxlaw/oberthodzi_zimbabwe_otjrdebates1.pdf.

Human Rights Watch. (2019). "Zimbabwe: Excessive Force Used Against Protestors". https://www.hrw.org/news/2019/03/12/zimbabwe-excessive-force-used-against-protesters.

Idang, Gabriel. (2015). "African Culture and Values", *Phronimon*, 16(2): 97–111. http://www.scielo.org.za/pdf/phronimon/v16n2/06.pdf (accessed September 27, 2021).

Jeater, Diana. (2016). "Masculinity, Marriage and the Bible: New Pentecostalist Masculinities in Zimbabwe", in Andrea Cornwall, Frank Karioris and Nancy Lindisfarne (eds.), *Masculinities Under Neoliberalism*. London: Zed Books, 165–182.

Karpowitz, Chrisopher, Mendelberg, Tali, and Shaker, Lee. (2012). "Gender Inequality in Deliberative Participation", *American Political Science Review*, 106 (3): 533–547. doi.org/10.1017/S0003055412000329.

King, Karen. (2003). *The Gospel of Mary of Magdala: Jesus and the First Woman Apostle*. Santa Rosa, CA: Polebridge Press.

Krook, Mona Lena. (2017). "Violence Against Women in Politics", *Journal of Democracy*, 28 (1): 74–88. www.journalofdemocracy.org/articles/violence-against-women-in-politics/.

Kugwa, Alfonce. (September 15, 2021). "Church on Women Empowerment Drive in the Fight Against Gender Based Violence", Catholic Church News Zimbabwe. Viewed from https://catholicchurchnewszimbabwe.wordpress.com/2021/09/15/church-on-women-empowerment-drive-in-the-fight-against-gender-based-violence/ [Date accessed September 29, 2021].

Mahmood, Saba. (2004). *Politics of Piety: The Islamic Revival and the Feminist Subject*. Princeton, NJ: Princeton University Press.

Manyonganise, Molly. (2015). "Women in Zimbabwe's War of 'Liberation': An Ethical Appraisal of the Sexual Conduct of Male Guerrillas", in

Fainos Mangena, Tarisayi Andrea Chimuka, Francis Mabiri (eds.), *Philosophy in African Traditions and Cultures: Zimbabwean Philosophical Studies, II*. Washington, DC: Council for Research in Value and Philosophy.

Marumo, Phelemo. (2016). "A Call for the Recognition and Empowerment of Women in Ministry in the Methodist Church of Southern Africa", *Studia Historiae Ecclesiasticae*, 42(3). dx.doi.org/10.17159/2412-4265/2016/1504.

McAfee, Nöelle. (2008). *Democracy and the Political Unconscious*. New York: Columbia University Press.

McNay, Lois. (2000). *Gender and Agency: Reconfiguring the Subject in Feminist and Social Theory*. Cambridge, MA: Polity Press.

Musodza, Blessing, Mapuranga, Barbra and Dumba, Oswald. (2015). "The Church and the Management of Gender Based Violence in Mutoko, Zimbabwe", *Public Policy and Administration Research*, 5 (10). https://core.ac.uk/download/pdf/234669816.pdf.

Muzambi, Prosper. (2018). "Cultural Alienation and Violence in Zimbabwean Politics: Some Lessons from the Ngozi Phenomenon", in Erasmus Masitera and Fortune Sibanda (eds.), *Power in Contemporary Zimbabwe*. London: Routledge.

Nakashina Brock, Rita, and Parker, Rebecca Ann. (2002). *Proverbs of Ashes: Violence, Redemptive Suffering, and the Search for What Saves Us*. Boston, MA: Beacon Press.

Oduyoye, Mercy Amba. (2005). *Daughters of Anowa*. Maryknoll, NY: Orbis Books.

Research and Advocacy Unit. (May 2010). "Women, Politics and the Zimbabwe Crisis", Report produced by Institute for Democratic Alternatives in South Africa, the International Centre for Transitional Justice, the Research and Advocacy Unit, and the Women's Coalition of Zimbabwe. Harare, Zimbabwe: Research and Advocacy Unit.

Research and Advocacy Unit and Zimbabwe Association of Doctors for Human Rights. (December 2010). "No Hiding Place: Politically Motivated Rape of Women in Zimbabwe". Viewed from www.archive.kubatana.net/docs/women/rau_zadhr_no_hiding_place_101209.pdf [Date accessed April 20, 2021].

Reuters Staff. (2020). "Zimbabwe Catholic Bishops, Lawyers Criticise Alleged Government Abuses", *Reuters*. Viewed from www.reuters.com/article/us-zimbabwe-politics-idUSKCN25C0NU [Date accessed August 12, 2022].

Schüssler Fiorenza, Elisabeth. (1983). *In Memory of Her: A Feminist Theological Reconstruction of Christian Origins*. New York: Crossroad.

Trible, Phyllis. (1984). *Texts of Terror: Literary-Feminist Readings of Biblical Narratives*. Minneapolis, MN: Fortress Press.

United Nations. (1993). *Declaration on the Elimination of Violence against Women*. Viewed from www.ohchr.org/en/professionalinterest/pages/violenceagainstwomen.aspx [Date accessed June 9, 2021].

World Health Organisation. (2021). "Violence against Women Fact Sheet". Viewed from www.who.int/news-room/fact-sheets/detail/violence-against-women [Date accessed June 9, 2021].

Zimbabwe Human Rights NGO Forum. (2006). "A Woman's Place is in the Home? Gender Based Violence and Opposition Politics in Zimbabwe". Viewed from http://humanrights.org.zw/bitstream/handle/123456789/369/Gender_%20Based_Violence_and_Opposition_Politics_in_Zimbabwe.pdf?sequence=1&isAllowed=y [Date accessed April 20, 2021].

Zimbabwe National Statistics Agency and ICF International. (2016). "Zimbabwe Demographic and Health Survey 2015: Final Report". Rockville, MD: Zimbabwe National Statistics Agency and ICF International. Viewed from https://dhsprogram.com/pubs/pdf/FR322/FR322.pdf [Dated accessed April 20, 2021].

Zydervelt, Sarah, Zajac, Rachel, Kaladelfos, Andy, and Westera, Nina. (May 2017). "Lawyers' Strategies for Cross-Examining Rape Complainants: Have We Moved Beyond the 1950s?" *British Journal of Criminology*, 57 (3): 551–569. doi.org/10.1093/bjc/azw023.

3
CASE STUDY 2: "GYAE MA NE NKA" (LET IT BE)

A Religious Notion of Peace or a Shutdown of Democratic Conversations?

3.1 Introduction

In every culture, there are norms and practices that are intended to promote a peaceful and stable society. These are sometimes drawn from religious texts, customs, or traditional beliefs and practices. *Gyae ma ne nka* is an example of such a phrase in Akan. Akan is one of the largest ethnic groups in West Africa, and the largest ethnic group in Ghana. Akan is also the language of the Akan people in Ghana. The use of the phrase, *gyae ma ne nka*, in this book mainly refers to usage in Ghana. *Gyae ma ne nka* translates as "let it be" or "let it go", and suggests "do not pursue an issue or do not seek redress". It is invoked in many diverse settings when there is an altercation, offence, or conflict between two or more parties, including within the family, in the community, and at the national and, potentially, international levels. It is employed by parents to "resolve" sibling quarrels; it is invoked by elders to "resolve" marital issues; and in political and corporate settings to diffuse potential disputes.

In many cultures, notions of *gyae ma ne nka* are intended to promote social cohesion. Godwin Etukumana (2020: 34) refers to African metaphors as an example of means and actions for

DOI: 10.4324/9781003214250-4

unification that bring about reconciliation and the restoration of the dignity of people. In Christian practices, *gyae ma ne nka* may advance forgiveness and suggest surrender to God. This manifestation of *gyae ma ne nka* does not operate in a vacuum. It leans on faith and lives in hope. More critically, it comes with a series of actions to ensure social harmony. Therefore, *gyae ma ne nka,* if invoked without the associated spaces for these interventions and support, could promote injustice and silence people, threaten the peace of the individual (a victim), and the stability of communities. This chapter proposes deliberative spaces in religion as a healthier approach to realising the intent behind g*yae ma ne nka* and to advance peace and stability.

3.2 Exploring the Essence of *Gyae ma ne nka*

Gyae ma ne nka has antecedents in many religions and cultures, particularly in Christianity. Examples of *gyae ma ne nka* are present in religious regions that also value a strong community bond such as in the Pacific Island Countries of Oceania, and in several communities in Africa. In such cultures, the practice of *gyae ma ne nka* is to promote peaceful co-existence in societies. It is touted as an elevated principle.

Apart from the need for peace and stability everywhere, in many Indigenous cultures, consideration for the other (or neighbour, generically) is deemed necessary for one's own sustenance. The Zulu (South African) word *Ubuntu*, which signifies the notion of "I am because you are", emphasises such oneness or unity (Thakhathi and Netshitangani 2020). This concept, widely recognised within Africa and beyond and used in everyday advice, idioms, and metaphors, provides some of the basis for *gyae ma ne nka*. Several African proverbs also reiterate the notion of *gyae ma ne nka*. In Ghana, the Akan proverb *ti koro nko agyina* (one head, or person does not hold counsel) places value on the collective. In Zimbabwe, the Shona proverb *kuziva mbuya huudzwa* (wisdom comes from others), stresses the need to consider the other. These underscore the fact that we are all in relationships with one another, and our state of well-being is a collective (Gyekye 1997). The traditional concept of destiny or predestination in Akan, *nkrabea,* suggests to people to leave things to take their course. This often implies a notion of patience and to let things be, *fa ma Nyame* (leave it to God.), or *Onyame asem* (it is God's business) (Pobee 1987: 45). Viewed within these laudable community principles, *gyae ma ne nka* is a practice that should help strengthen families and communities.

In a conversation with Ghanaian theologian, lawyer, women's advocate and counsellor, Angela Dwamena-Aboagye (November 18, 2021), she explained that, traditionally, the use of *gyae ma ne nka* is not arbitrary. There are times when traditional leaders have found it necessary to encourage disputants to let it go. For instance, in a case at the chief's court, when Nana (the chief) has satisfied himself of a fair hearing, weighed the options and impact on the greater good and sometimes even the long-term well-being of the offended, Nana may say, *m'atu me nae asi asem yi so* (literally meaning he has placed his foot on this matter), and the inherent advice is "it is better for you to let it go"; it is not necessary to pursue the case. The general public may not see all the counsel that went into the decision, but the advice or ruling would not be arbitrary.

Therefore, at its best, *gyae ma ne nka* is intended to prevent persistent grudges which, in an interconnected society, could stigmatise the offender. To avoid social stigmatisation, it is important that victims forgive or let go; otherwise, like the lepers of the Hebrew Bible and ancient African society, the offenders could be perceived as outcasts. Unfortunately, within this communal intent, the victim, when they refuse to let go, could also be stigmatised as a family-wrecker, community-breaker, self-centred, and self-serving individual. Within the context of purity, the victim could be seen to be tarnishing the reputation of the community (be it Christian, Indigenous, or other forms of community). To refuse to let go, when asked to do so, could cause embarrassment or bring disgrace to individuals, families, and communities, and potentially break relational ties. To a large extent, then, the reasons for invoking *gyae ma ne nka* do not necessarily or always relate directly to the offence committed or to the offended person or victim. It is often in the interest of "peace and stability" of the community, relationship, or family. But who gets to invoke *gyae ma ne nka*?

Gyae ma ne nka has inherent power dynamics. It is pervasive, gendered, and stratified. In practice, it is often persons of a lower status in society or marginalised groups who are advised to let go or let it be. This includes women, young people, the poor, and persons of low status in society. The practice tends to favour the rich, influential, and powerful and mostly men in society. It is not unusual to hear the low in status advised to let it be because the perpetrator is too powerful, or too prominent to have their reputation tarnished. The everyday reasoning behind this "intervention" sounds somewhat like, "let go because he/she is too powerful for you to battle"; "let go, otherwise you will destroy the unity in the family or the community"; "let go for the sake of the marriage or the children". The reasons for *gyae ma ne nka* are mostly "other-centred", but not necessarily altruistic.

In patriarchal societies, women are especially told to let go. *Gyae ma ne nka* features prominently in cases of domestic violence or spousal abuse. As the founder of the first national shelter for battered women in Ghana (the Ark Foundation), Angela Dwamena-Aboagye observed in the conversation cited above that many abused women are pressured to drop the cases in favour of family unity. For these women, the court system is expensive and cumbersome, and the fear of retribution from society does not make it easy to pursue justice. Ramphele (2017: 121) observes that "patriarchy runs in the veins of all the cultures of our society; constitutional requirements of gender equality have yet to find expression in our homes, places of work, schools and religious institutions", adding that "hierarchical relationships frame the institutional cultures of a significant majority". The implication is that often the less powerful person cannot seek justice. Pre-conditioned by notions of predestination, Pobee (1987) posits that letting things be in African Traditional Religion (ATR) and society substantially contributes to the inability to promptly check tyranny. Often, it is convenient for those who have benefited from the offence to say let it go without the work that it entails. This is reminiscent of the perspectives some hold on issues of slavery and reparations.

The challenge is that over time, a victim (or survivor), might be more offended, rejected, and abused. They may react, and do so violently, thereby disturbing the peace that was intended by *gyae ma ne nka*. The Akan proverb, *ɛtaa aponkyene a, okye wuɔ* (literally meaning when the goat chokes, it vomits), explains what occurs within a victim of abuse. When they can no longer handle the suppression of their voices, they erupt. While researching this book, we learned about the story of a mother of three adult girls who was also a wife until recently. For 40 years she was married to her then-husband and encountered many abusive issues that were never resolved. When she complained to family elders, and church leaders, she was told "don't worry, it will pass", "every marriage has issues", "consider the children". While this reasoning may be true, it need not be at her expense, nor should it preclude the concerns she presented. She endured these issues which resulted in substantial and harmful emotional and mental abuse. She left the marriage after 40 years when her children were out of home and mostly married. She is a happier woman now. Could such prolonged trauma in these four decades have been avoided? This woman is arguably one of the fortunate in such cases of domestic abuse. Spouses and intimate partners, predominantly women, lose their lives either from direct violence or from poor quality of life, and in some cases, commit suicide. If they live, they may contract stress-related diseases or end up in prison for maiming or murdering an abusive spouse or intimate partner.

When people who have been offended are *simply* told to let it be, two possible scenarios may occur in parallel:

- The offended are asked to make further sacrifices by letting go. The intervention does not cater to their needs—physical, emotional, or psychological.
- The offenders are not likely to be held accountable, partly because the attitude that the offended is asked to assume relieves the perpetrator of much responsibility. The process leaves the offended hopeless and helpless.

In our case study of political violence against women in chapter two, many victims observed that when they report abuse to authorities, they are told that women's issues were not at the top of the government's agenda; there will be a time to discuss such issues and the time is yet to come, although it often doesn't come and is overtaken by other national priorities. Implicit in this "advice" is that the victims can "park" the issue, and by extension, let go for the moment. There is no sense of urgency, partly due to the lack of appropriate and adequate infrastructure, but also these cases are hushed by a cultural practice that is abused to the detriment of the marginalised. The result is suppressed pain, and trans-generational trauma, whereas processes of redress and healing as Gobodo-Madikizela (2020) describes could help break the transmissions of vicious cycles of the past.

The case of the *State v. Lakela Sweswe* in Zimbabwe is instructive here.

> A young woman murdered her husband after allegedly living with continuous abuse by him, especially when he came home drunk. On the night in question her husband was drunk and had beaten her up, threatened to stab her and then left. Upon his return, she stabbed him on his neck as he entered the bedroom; he fell to the ground and was immobile. She poured water on him and tried to lift him up but couldn't, so she left him there and he bled to death. She spent two days with the body and when it started to decompose, she doused it with paraffin, burnt it then ran away from her homestead.
>
> In the trial, the young woman used self-defence suggesting that she thought her husband had gone to get a lethal weapon to kill her so she stabbed him first. The court acknowledged the domestic violence in her marriage and on the fateful night but refused to accept her self-defence plea as she didn't seek help after stabbing her husband. *"She, unfortunately, decided to take matters into her own hands. It is regrettable that a life was needlessly lost",* the court sentence stated (S v Lakela Sweswe HC (CRB) 67/18). She was found guilty of murder and sentenced to 18 years in prison. Police accounts suggested that this woman had lodged reports about abuse from the husband a few times. She may have failed to see the domestic violence

case through for fear of losing the family breadwinner, her husband and fear of being accused of dishonouring her husband. The point is, she did not receive the help she needed.

Perspectives on *gyae ma ne nka* may vary based on identity and interests. These include: (a) gender, as the practices of *gyae ma ne nka* tends to affect men and women differently in Africa; (b) age—persons above 60 years may be more accepting of *gyae ma ne nka* as their immersion into their cultures are likely deeper than younger generations; (c) religious leaders, particularly with theologies that favour forgiveness; (d) peace and development practitioners/democratic actors who straddle a spectrum of processes for mediation and negotiation as well as the pursuit of justice and reconciliation; (e) traditional leaders/traditionalists, some of whom may uphold the tenets of *gyae ma ne nka* while others may favour "an arm for an arm; a tooth for a tooth" practice; and (f) the states and governments whose attempt to establish democratic institutions are infused with more cultural considerations than are perhaps acknowledged.

3.3 The Notion of "Let It Be" in Religious Practices: A Look at Traditional Practices and Christianity

A review of *gyae ma ne nka* within religion and culture is instructive in understanding the nuances of the practice in Africa. While both religion and culture are intricately connected as practices, the interest here is to determine the extent to which one influences the other in the practice of *gyae ma ne nka*. In most African societies there is a fusion between traditional practices and religious expectations resulting in a widely acceptable norm of "letting go" that promotes peace. Or does it? Could it be that the practice of *gyae ma ne nka* in Christianity had no resistance because the notions of "let it be" already existed in African culture?

Gyae ma ne nka has a notion of forgiveness. In Christian practices, the call for forgiveness is referenced in the Lord's Prayer: "Forgive us our sins, for we ourselves forgive everyone indebted to us" (Luke 11:4, NRSV). There is an element of reciprocity—giving and receiving. Forgiveness in Christian terms also suggests the "battle is the Lord's" (2 Chronicles 20:15; 1 Samuel 17:47). There is also an element of surrender. The promise Christians have is that a higher power—God—will take care of the problem. Furthermore, surrender to God and "letting go" of the grudge is the premise for peace (Philippians 4:6–7). In the interview with Angela Dwamena-Aboagye, she adds that in Christianity, *gyae ma ne nka*, as forgiveness, is a practice of faith and Christians are encouraged to let go, especially since they have received greater forgiveness from Christ through the work of salvation. It is a practice that advances the inner peace of the individual. She notes, however, that in both traditional and Christian settings, *gya ma ne nka* should not be an imposition but a decision of the individual. They can and should be aided to arrive at that decision as an option to free the mind and heart of the burden of offence. She also indicates that such a decision does not prevent the reporting or pursuance of a criminal offence. So *gyae ma ne nka*, as intended in this Christian context, does not leave issues in vacuum. It comes with a series of actions (practices). People need help to reflect on the journey towards letting it be. While these norms potentially existed in the culture predating Christianity, there is no doubt that there have been mutual influences from traditions and Christian practices.

Gyae ma ne nka is carried through various cultural and traditional customs in different ethnic groups. Among the Ashantis and most of the Akans in Ghana, *mpata* is a practice conducted when a perpetrator of an offence recognises and admits to an offence and seeks restitution. *Mpata* does not necessarily solve the problem. The offended or victim is expected to drop the case (let go) once the perpetrator admits guilt and seeks forgiveness. It is not a conversation or dialogue between the two parties. Rather, elders or respected members of the society conduct the conversation and often present gifts as appeasement to the offended. Do victims find peace through the peace offering? If the offended refuse to accept the *mpata*, they then become the ones perceived to be breaking up society. In parts of Northern Ghana, when a person of prominent status in the community "holds the leg" of their victim in an altercation, the latter is expected to let the matter rest. These gestures are also common in cases of marital disputes. Kneeling to touch the leg or feet is deemed an act of humility. The offender has literally "gone low" to seek forgiveness.

In Akan, there are subtle references to mediation within *gyae ma ne nka*. The phrase *wo de dwantua* suggests an intervener or a process requiring mediation. Aligned with Christian teaching, Jesus is seen as a mediator. The Akans therefore say, "Yesu, yɛ dwantua hene" (Jesus is King of mediation)—one who plays a mediatory role. Within the practice of *gyae ma ne nka*, however, while this is presented as mediation, the intent is to let it go. The challenge is it is often particular groups of people that are expected to let go, especially women, young people, or the vulnerable in society, without an improvement in the issues that affected them.

3.4 The Morals of *Gyae ma ne nka* and the Decadence of Religious Spaces

In religious regions, such as Africa and Oceania, the relationship between individuals, families, and communities on the one hand, and their religious leaders, institutions and structures on the other, is one that is revered. The church in such places could be a space to seek faith and hope, seek support and community, and particularly seek prayers and sometimes miracles. It is highly likely that a troubled person will speak to their pastor about a problem first, before the family. The notion of going to a family pastor, minister, or priest is common.

These religious spaces also serve as places to seek advice and redress. In addition to pastors or ministers, groups, associations, and guilds also provide platforms for support.

In her book, *Ministering to the Hurting: Women's Mental Health and Pastoral Response in Ghana* (2021), theologian and gender advocate Angela Dwamena-Aboagye observes that in Christian settings, pastors (both men and women, but for a long time they were exclusively men in many societies across the world), are often front line responders when women in their churches are in crisis. She provides insights based on stories of ten Ghanaian women, her own mental health journey, and interviews with a number of pastors in

Pentecostal churches in Ghana. There is no doubt that some people have received sound, life-saving advice and protection in these spaces. But what happens when religion is ambivalent in cases of injustice, discrimination, and abuse? Dwamena-Aboagye also raises concerns about the capacity and competence of pastors to appreciate the full dimensions of such issues. What if they *simply* ask the offended to forgive and let go?

Is *gyae ma ne nka* forgiveness? And if it is, at whose expense? In many parts of West Africa and South Eastern Africa, cultural identity determines, to a great extent, how forgiveness and reconciliation are processed. Theological understandings of forgiveness vary even within Christianity. Professor of public theology and ethics at Stellenbosch University in South Africa, Dion A. Forster's inquiry regarding the complexities of religion, race and politics in South Africa is instructive (2020). Based on a four-year empirical study, he observes that among White South Africans, forgiveness tends to be an individualised and spiritualised endeavour. Black South Africans tend to see forgiveness as social and spiritual well-being within a community, manifesting in economic and social justice. He calls this the Politics of Forgiveness (Forster 2018). While forgiveness is an important part of being a Christian, Forster observes that there are some aspects of forgiveness that are theologically untrue and politically problematic. They are thin conceptualisations of forgiveness. These are not healing and transformative and do not reconcile communities. These notions of forgiveness are sometimes interpreted as a confession of the individual to God. They seek forgiveness from God, and God forgives them. This conceptualisation does not always factor in the trauma a victim may have suffered and the actions needed for restorative justice. Forster suggests that forgiveness has both a conceptual element (What is forgiveness?) as well as a social state (What does forgiveness look like?). In his works, he enquires whether forgiveness could be a weapon that further wounds Black South Africans to the extent that they are not only to live with the social, political, and economic consequences of Apartheid, but also to stop calling for justice. Forster (2020) recalls Nathan Trantraal's poem that speaks of how the Christian religion calls on Black South Africans to forgive, without always counting the cost of the call for forgiveness. Trantraal (2017; in Forster, 2020: 51) speaks of the poison in forgiveness (*die gif in vergifnis*). When the wounded, hurt or abused is further asked to sacrifice to address the needs of perpetrators or other observers of the community, it does not just condone the offence but also silences the victim's voice. Inferring from biblical teachings, forgiveness should precipitate a change in behaviour, sometimes triggered by transformative justice. When people choose to forgive, the circumstances that caused their pain or challenges do not go away automatically.

A different set of interventions might help to change the circumstances that caused the pain. In places like South Africa, people, particularly those disadvantaged by Apartheid, are not just looking for social cohesion: they are looking for solutions that guarantee economic prosperity, justice, and equality. They are looking for structural transformation. "I can't eat forgiveness," observed Kayla, a young, social justice-driven, White South African student who is aware of and engaged in the realities and consequences of Apartheid (Conversation May 2021). She further explains that it is not enough to tell people to forgive. If the pain and trauma of the past continues to cause hunger, and there are no measures to mitigate the struggle, we cause more pain. She considers the church and religious organisations complicit in this matter. Kayla considers the Christian narrative to be one of "forgiveness before anger". Reflecting on the Truth and Reconciliation Commission of South Africa, she observed that multitudes of people who had something to say were not factored into the process, describing them as "the people left behind by forgiveness", left behind by "let's move forward", she adds. Kayla's frustration, she reckons, resonates with many of her generation.

The paradox of "moving forward" while implying "left behind" is instructive here. It raises questions of who got involved in the "moving forward" agenda, how they arrived at the decision and action to let go and/or move forward and to what extent they participated in and owned the process. What are the efforts to address the challenges that caused the offence or pain? These are the questions that challenge key ethical practices like *Ubuntu* in Africa (Maris 2020; Bewaji and Ramose 2003).

Letting go is a process, just as forgiveness ought to be a process of healing. As Dwamena-Aboagye explains in the conversation cited above, in Christian teachings Jesus did not just let it go. There were many instances of confronting social injustice. It was costly, but also catered to the needy and underprivileged. She suggests that the sociocultural factors that suppress people, especially where there is power imbalance, ought to be confronted; otherwise, a simple *gyae ma ne nka* worsens the pain of the oppressed. The practice of *gyae ma ne nka*, when not accompanied by spaces that welcome the expression of concerns, could silence voices under the pretext of promoting forgiveness, peace, and social cohesion.

Although the phrase *gyae ma ne nka* isn't common in a European and US context, the idea is present. For example, in September 2018, in Dallas, Texas, a White police officer named Amber Guyger killed her unarmed Black neighbour, Botham Jean, in his own home while he sat on his couch having ice cream. Botham was an accountant, a graduate of Harding University, and an immigrant to the United States from Saint Lucia. Guyger later, implausibly, claimed that she thought she was in her own apartment and that he was an intruder—even though the apartment was on another floor with different furnishings. At the trial, Jean's brother, Brant Jean, asked to hug his brother's murderer and said that he forgave her. The video and account of this went viral. While many honoured the choices and actions of the victim's brother, there was also concern that this particular story was highlighted by many and went viral because it was an appealing account of a Black person forgiving and letting go of anger, hostility, hurt, and trauma related to the systematic violence of White people against Black people and immigrants. This example raises questions about who society expects to "let go" and move on? Cornell Brooks, former National Association for the Advancement of Colored People (NAACP) President and African Methodist Episcopal minister highlighted this concern, noting that he has "preached forgiveness for 25 years", but that "using the willingness of Black people to forgive as an excuse to further victimize Black people is SINFUL. America should ask Black people for forgiveness for serially asking African Americans to forgive sanctioned Police Brutality" (Brooks 2019).

This example, among so many others, leads us to ask, What is the cost of *gyae ma ne nka*? *Gyae ma ne nka* as forgiveness has consequences. Does the practice deprive others in the same community of their own sense of community and peace? Does the current application of the practice deviate from the intended goals of our predecessors and ancestors? This inquiry is less about the appropriateness of the notion of *gyae ma ne nka*, and more about how the concept is carried out. In spite of its intended purpose and potential for unity, *gyae ma ne nka* as forgiveness and letting go, if pursued without the necessary spaces for expressions, could stop the offended from pursuing any course of redress, including healing and restoration, and could alienate persons from the very communities they are expected to sustain. If the concept is to enforce Christian forgiveness, how might it be made authentic and how could it promote community building? For some, forgiveness often requires acknowledgement from the offender, doused in a good offer of mercy from the offended. Both Christian and African practices of forgiveness, mercy or any iteration of *gyae ma ne nka* need not preclude redress. A core feature of peace and reconciliation processes, which *gyae ma ne nka* espouses, is to create space for those affected to articulate their grievances. As Dwamena-Aboagye suggests in the conversation mentioned above, the church has a shepherding role and shepherds tend their flock. God invites us to a conversation that activates the role of the shepherd. It is perhaps the absence of adequate mutually satisfactory spaces for talking through issues that poses the challenge. Most times the inability to hear and address the concerns of the other reinforces the hurt and creates "a historical knot", or a frozen conflict. Perhaps it is the complexity of conflict resolution and the risk of opening a pandora's box (and fear of the content fracturing community) that people are quickly asked to let go. The silence, on the other hand, does not necessarily restore relationships. The absence of healthy spaces to address issues could create a victim who is wounded in multiple ways, and a perpetrator who will most likely commit the offence again, as they can get away with it.

The point here is that while intended for peace and stability, *gyae ma ne nka*, or the "let it be" peace attitude can threaten peace itself. First, it threatens the inner peace of the individual, and then peace towards others. Contrary to its intended purpose, the expected serenity and stability of "let it be" could unleash violence upon people who have been wronged, particularly those at the receiving end of injustice. The expectation that people who have been unfairly treated would "normalise" and move on could in itself be violating. This is particularly so if the offended do not find spaces to process the experience. "Let it be", when it shuts down a process for finding solutions, could have the reverse impact. It can potentially be an abusive peace process and not truly reconciliatory. Here, we acknowledge the extensive work on what forgiveness should be or the shortcomings, including the intersections of forgiveness and mercy, justice, and redemption. That is not our inquiry. We propose deliberative spaces as a platform for realising the intentions of *gyae ma ne nka*, including useful and just iterations of forgiveness, and the possibility of a shared sense of direction.

3.5 "Let It Be": Peace and Social Injustice in Traditional and Religious Spaces

Intended to promote social cohesion, concepts like *gyae ma ne nka* have been abused and in the process have undermined justice and peace. Forgiveness does not necessarily lead to reconciliation or harmony. In the conversation with Dion Forster mentioned earlier (November 2021), he shared two insights from his research on forgiveness. First, forgiveness is abused when applied in a utilitarian manner. This is because forgiveness becomes a short-term goal which hardly solves the underlying problem. Second, forgiveness is abused when it is used as a signifier and used by the powerful or persons of influence to attach moral values. Invokers of *gyae ma ne nka* may use phrases like "we are Christians, we must let go". He observes that in such instances, one ought to reflect on the context within which forgiveness is requested or suggested and who is asking us to do so. He adds that it is often by people who benefit from the status quo. It is not always a call on the tenets of their faith.

The transactional nature of the concept of forgiveness and the expectation it places on those who have been wronged raises issues of injustice and concerns over the strength of the community

(Gobodo-Madikizela 2003). Within the scope of SDG 16 (Target 16.7.2), which refers to the "proportion of population who believe decision-making is inclusive and responsive, by sex, age, disability and population group", people involved in an altercation or anything that affects them ought to feel part of the decisions in ways that are healing and restorative. As both John W. de Gruchy (2002) and Dion Foster (2018, 2019b) suggest, reconciliation presents an opportunity for the parties to face each other in conversation for meaningful inter-group contact; reconciliation cannot be pursued without the alienated parties facing each other.

In her chapter on "*Ubuntu* as a Healing Framework", South African political thinker/activist, academic and medical doctor, Mamphela Ramphele, asks how we can use *Ubuntu* as a philosophical standpoint to heal. In her explanation of *Ubuntu* idealism, she observes that "my humanity is co-substantially bestowed upon the other and me. Humanity is a quality we owe to each other" (2017: 108). She further suggests that this notion "imposes an inescapable ethical and moral code on our relationships" (108). This interconnectedness and interdependence suggest that "the oppressor is the mirror of the oppressed" (109). She submits that *Ubuntu* provides an avenue to restore our connectedness when it is broken by oppression. While *Ubuntu*'s approach to justice is conciliatory rather than punitive, the process requires face-to face encounters that allow reconnection in safe and supportive spaces (110). She explains that in traditional societies, family members and persons of significance in the society, accompany both the offender and the offended as they attend the conversations. In most Ghanaian cultural settings, the persons who accompany the parties are described as "one with a heavy face", suggesting a respected personage. In keeping with the spirit of *Ubuntu*, wrongdoing to one member of the family or clan is an affront to the entire family. *Ubuntu*, Ramphele explains, therefore advocates dignity, compassion, and humanness, and causes a shift from confrontation and vengeance to mediation and conciliation (112). In these spaces, forgiveness is expected to be requested (by the wrongdoer) and forgiveness is expected to be given (by the wronged). However, this requires processes, conversations, and safe spaces. Ramphele suggests that people go into the process of conciliation expecting full disclosure and closure (2017: 110). Referring to South Africa's conciliatory process, she suggests that both top-down and bottom-up processes are needed to surface social injustice and address psychosocial and interpersonal justice. She observes "healing cannot be sustained unless there is a holistic approach that involves conversations at all levels of society": conversations that allow citizens to share their stories and make way for mutual understanding and affirmation (111).

Gyae ma ne nka, without the necessary processing, creates a suppressed sentiment of injustice and, over time, breeds discontented people in the community and even in the church. The difference or perhaps the connection that should exist between forgiveness and *gyae ma ne nka* is a sense of responsibility and mediating steps that heal and develop communities. The notion of mediation is present in Christian texts. In Matthew 18: 15–17, Jesus lays out a process by which mediators should be brought in to talk through issues. This implies deliberative spaces, where more than the two parties involved will hear the perspectives and find a good solution. It is also remarkable that the process involves the offender and the offended.

Should we give up on the pursuit of *gyae ma ne nka?*. As indicated, *gyae ma ne nka* is often well-intentioned in cultures that apply it. Yet, it has been abused in self-serving ways, supported by power imbalances, the quest for in-group identity, and the desire for quick solutions. The question then is, what are the framings of forgiveness, *gyae ma ne nka*, and "letting go" that we ought to give up? Forster, in various publications (2018, 2019a, 2019b, 2020), suggests forgiveness that does not dehumanise the other, and forgiveness that is able to look into the past in order to move into the future. Deliberative democratic practices may suggest *gyae ma ne nka* or letting go that invites people to name and frame the issues while learning about others' perspectives on the matter, even if their perspectives are difficult to hear or contradict our own experiences and views. How do we create spaces in which we encounter the other as a fellow human being? How do we learn about the issues behind the issue in a healthy conversation?

3.6 Promoting *Gyae ma ne nka* through Democratic Practices

If *gyae ma ne nka*, manifesting as forgiveness in the church or as unity in African culture, is to promote peace, then the practice needs to reinforce openness and conciliation. These principles promote fairness and justice. They will also reignite the wisdom behind these practices as the forefathers and foremothers intended. Such traditional wisdom will consider the timing for *gyae ma ne nka*. It should consider who gets involved in the process. Parties ought to understand or at least appreciate or respond to the question, "Letting go for what?" What specifically are they letting go? Perhaps to allow new love to grow, perhaps to enable new energies to emerge in relationships, perhaps to be able to change the narrative? In many ways *gyae ma ne nka* is used metaphorically. It is layered. It needs to be unpacked through conversations to prevent misinterpretation and misapplication. To advance the overarching goals of *gyae ma ne nka*, namely valuing community, demonstrating love in justice, and thinking of others, it may be useful to take a step back for reflective learning. How have these practices been carried out? To advance these ideals, there ought to be spaces for conversation, for curiosity, and for learning from one another. Democratic practices, like religious practices as outlined in chapter one, offer practical steps.

Religious spaces have a significant impact on community cohesion. Such spaces need their members for the necessary work of community building. If churches, for instance, were to reassess their processes of forgiveness and other religious traditions that invoke notions of *gyae ma ne nka* in ways that are mutually beneficial to all concerned, social cohesion is more likely to be realised. What might make *gyae ma ne nka* realise its full potential as intended in Akan communities and the rest of Africa, as well as cultures that uphold the oneness of community? Rather than shut down voices and perspectives, how might the practice of *gyae ma ne nka* create a deliberative process that gives voice to the offended and gives room for the offended to weigh the options available. This way, when people let go, they do so in full glare of the options available to both them and the community. They would have carefully considered the trade-offs and the consequences that may come with their choice. The point is that "let it be" is not a passive practice. It involves a series of efforts—practices that result in lasting peace and stronger communities. Failing that, people are "forced" to be quiet. In reality, they hardly let it be. The issue is likely to re-emerge in the community, often with even more damaging consequences. Opening up spaces to address the problems, also opens up options towards restoration.

As actors in civil society, religious groups have played a critical role in socioeconomic development and political transformations. In Ghana, the involvement of the Christian Council of Churches, the Pentecostal Council and Catholic Conferences as well as the office of the National Chief Imam, among other religious institutions, in ensuring successive electoral transitions and peaceful elections has been and remains significant. In other parts of Africa, the important role of churches can be seen in Mozambique's journey from war to peace (Schubert 2013: 112–136), and certainly in South Africa's political transformation (Kusmierz and Cochrane 2013: 49–84). Religion has the potential to provide a broader language by which faith groups can work out differences and strengthen democracy. We also see examples of how traditional authorities have used their "good offices" to advance democratic practices. The role of the Asantehene in Ghana's governance and peace processes is instructive in this regard. Rather than introducing a "foreign" idea of democratic practice to Indigenous and religious traditions around *gyae ma ne nka*, deliberative democratic spaces and practices rejuvenate the original intent of *gyae ma ne nka*. It provides a process that leads people beyond an offence, to community building and sustained collective action needed for democratic development.

Jeffrey Stout observes that freedom of religion, which is enshrined in many constitutions, consists of the right to make up one's own mind in ways that seem appropriate, provided that these do not harm others (2004: 63). The theory and practice of deliberation varies across cultures, evidenced by ancient African decision-making processes, such as those observed in ancient Egyptian hieroglyphics and the *talanoa* or the *hui* of Oceania. There are countless examples and a strong case to be made that there is a natural instinct of human beings to deliberate and make informed decisions together. With careful observation and attention, we see that this trait is present in everyday lives and does not require professional or expert skills or training. Jane Mansbridge (2012) explains this in her notion of the deliberative system. She observes that the deliberative system includes everyday talk on what people consider important to discuss in both private and public spaces. Religious groups offer activities both in so-called personal spaces, as well as in public spaces. The deliberative system helps its participants understand themselves and their environments better. In many ways, religious groups can offer these spaces in guilds and associations, cell groups, Bible classes, and other meetings where deliberation and decision-making are central features of the group. These conversations are opportunities for change, "as doers of the Word".

For most deliberative democracy theorists, such talks or conversations ought to lead to binding actions (Gutman and Thompson 2004). But this is not always visible or tangible. The shift in ideas and the actions they may prompt in deliberative work is not always seen or really observable. Mansbridge (2012) argues that everyday talks produce results collectively, even if not at the same time and in the same space within a specified time. Everyday talk is one part of the spectrum and the start of formalised decision-making spaces. In other words, no formal public forum occurs in a vacuum. People would have engaged the subject at kitchen tables, barbershops, salons, and markets. In his book, the *Ecology of Democracy*, David Mathews buttresses this point when he observes, "Not all deliberation occurs in forums. People make decisions together every day in the political wetlands, and deliberative moments are mixed into ordinary conversations" (Mathews, 2014: 79). In many African cities, if you were to ask how someone was doing (a greeting of well-being), they are likely to respond with a slight commentary on the sociopolitical or economic system. A typical working-class dialogue in Accra is likely to ring as such:

Menua, ɛte sɛn? (My brother/sister, how are things?)
Onyame Adom oo (By God's Grace); Na woɛ? (and you?)

Hmm, enuoma mu ayɛ
den (Things are difficult.)

Dollar no a kɔ soro (The US dollar has appreciated against the Ghana cedi, [implying higher prices or cost of imports or inflation]).

In those few by-the-roadside greetings, there has been a reflection on a challenging economy, doused by a dose of reference to the Divine. The participants have expressed their concerns and issues have been identified and framed in ways that resonate with those concerned. This is not an expert framing. The issue is framed in public terms, and in how ordinary citizens perceive that concern. This perspective is important if those "ordinary citizens" or everyday people are expected to be part of the solution. Their perspectives ought to be heard.

Deliberation aims at action and collectively binding decisions. Mansbridge (2012) argues that the concept of public reasoning goes beyond pure rationality to a considered level of a mix of emotions. Even when people are silent, their silence speaks and shapes the conversation either by indicating nonchalance, oppressiveness, lack of interest, boredom, or confusion. This fits within family, community, religious as well as public conversations. It does not only exclude the level of rational decision-making required in public deliberation but also does not ignore the characteristics of everyday talk.

The Fear of Religion and Politics

In most of Africa, as it is in many parts of the world, the understanding of "politics" tends to highlight partisanship, marked by elections and politicians. Within this understanding, it is common to hear people observe, "I do not do politics", or "I do not want to get involved in politics". Yet, what they mean is that they do not engage in partisan politics, or do not want to be aligned to any political ideology or political party. As noted in earlier chapters, they *do* make choices in everyday life, based on what they consider to be the best choice at a given time, within a set of circumstances and cannot fully escape "politics", as understood more broadly. Politics is ultimately choice-making, and it involves a broader range of thoughts and practices than partisanship. Highlighting that the personal is political, Mansbridge points out that the everyday, informal forms of action and deliberation are best understood as political. She observes:

> I propose that we define as political "that which the public ought to discuss", when that discussion forms part of some, perhaps highly informal, version of a collective "decision". As a collective, we the people... make many more "decisions" than appear in our formal state apparatus. Large numbers of mutually interacting individual choices weighted unequally... together create a host of collective choices. Those collective choices or "decisions", then affect, often substantially, the individual choices of each member of the collective.
>
> *(2012: 89)*

She considered this formulation more specific than Habermas' "matters of general interest" (1979: 49) or Benhabib's "matters of common concern" (1994: 26). These conversations or decisions, even though not made in concert, could eventually shape public decisions and state policies as they trickle down through individuals that form religious groups into their professional and societal spaces, and affect most people in the polity.

When "the personal is political" is analysed within the framework of *gyae ma ne nka*, we understand that consideration for the collective is the reason individuals are advised to let go. Could this same consideration for the collective be the same reason why individual voices should be heard?

Gyae ma ne nka *and Deliberative Democracy*

In this book, we have been concerned with the voices of the people in religious spaces. In the preface to his 1995 book *Learning to Speak: The Church's Voice in Public Affairs*, Keith Clements describes the many instances where the church is asked to take a prophetic stand on issues. Yet, others have criticised the church for "talking" too much. When the church speaks for its people, it often "calls" for an action or encourages its members to let it go or act in a certain way, often towards social cohesion. Where exactly does one locate the voices of the people? As a critical non-state actor, could religious spaces be more collaborative, consultative, and cooperative? Within the context of the SDGs (Target 16.7), could religious groups have more "responsive, inclusive, participatory and representative decision-making at all levels" and could deliberative practices help to "broaden and strengthen the participation" (Target 16.8)?

As discussed in chapter one, deliberative democracy offers several practices that map onto many religious practices. Given the resonances in several African practices and religion, we also see deliberative practices that find expression in African culture. This section offers a more "how to" approach to practising *gyae ma ne nka* that makes religious spaces safer and more healing, participatory, and inclusive.

Citizens are not just beneficiaries or consumers. For this reason, citizens cannot be left on the sidelines (Mathews 2014: 63). Their work is needed to complement that of governments, schools, and even churches. Elinor Ostrom, arguing for a citizen-centred democracy suggests,

> Ignoring the important role of children, families, support groups, neighbourhood organisations, and churches in the production of [public] services means... that only a portion of the inputs to these processes are taken into account in the way that policymakers think about these problems.
>
> *(1993: 8)*

She suggests people should be seen not as clients, but as co-producers. Client is a passive role while a co-producer makes one an active partner. To this extent, what citizens do can supplement what institutions do or complement what officials cannot do or will not do. Mathews describes this as "complementary production" (2014: 64). In the church, beyond being part of the congregation, these persons are citizens in the sense described above, and beyond being part of the citizenry, some are professionals with specialised skills and knowledge, and at the very least, knowledge of their own circumstances and what they value. If those to whom religious groups cater are co-producers, they ought to inform decision-making around issues that affect them. They ought to be able to name the issues in ways that are meaningful to them. This is not only for ethical, moral, or theological reasons, but also for highly practical reasons: when people are involved in naming and framing issues of importance to them and deliberating on the way forward, they are more likely to be a productive and meaningful part of addressing such issues. If *gyae ma ne nka* is a call to let go, and if it manifests as forgiveness in the church, then how might the church approach this in ways that those offended in particular, but also all parties involved, could be part of the processes that enable a peaceful and sound *gyae ma ne nka*?

(Re)Framing the Process of *Gyae ma ne nka*

a) Identifying the issue?

Gyae ma ne nka is invoked when there is an issue. It is not in vacuum. The invocation also suggests that someone, or at least one party, is concerned about a problem, and most likely hurt or offended by some incident. How the affected person names that problem has implications for their willingness to let go. As in any conflict, the parties involved may not see the issue in the same way. If a mediator suggests to one party to let go, without the party having the opportunity to "work through" the problem, the chances of totally letting go will be slim; and where *gyae ma ne nka* is understood as forgiveness without the necessary considerations, there will be internalised grievances, particularly where the offender does not acknowledge the offence.

b) Unearthing concerns

When people are simply told to let go, we have missed an opportunity to journey with them to understand their pain; working through that pain allows them to forgive or let go. We have missed their perspectives on the matter if we did not allow them to process their concerns. In deliberative practices, the notion of framing an issue provides an opportunity for persons to name what bothers them, and hear the perspectives of other people. In a deliberative *gyae ma ne nka* process, we could find shared concerns. This generates paths for options towards joint solutions. When we collectively frame the issue at stake, various parties may see their concerns considered, and may be more open to solutions.

c) The search for collective solutions and actions

In addition to naming their concerns, it is important that parties are given the opportunity to "appear" and to talk through their fears, anxieties, and trauma (Oelofson 2020). In public deliberation, a key feature of deliberative democracy, people get to exercise judgement. This is not a decision imposed on them, but one they arrived at because they talked through the problem and considered the options available to them, as well as the trade-offs associated with each decision and line of action. (Yankelovich 1991). Among religious groups, the considerations may involve their faith and sacred scriptures. Mathews suggests that "a judgement is said to be sound if it is consistent with what we consider most valuable in a particular situation" (2014: 73). He describes this as "choice work" (78). Here, deliberation is distinct from a mere discussion or debates that can degenerate into binary divides and sore arguments. At its best, deliberation and the process of working through available options to make a choice enable people to grapple with tensions, and areas where they disagree with others. Within the context of ATR and practices, the considerations will go beyond the bare facts of the case, to considerations about cultural demands, family, and community well-being. That is an African Deliberative System. With a good sense of the consequences of each approach to solution, *gyae ma ne nka* then becomes an informed choice, and those who let go may even work collaboratively to prevent future occurrences, or promote community cohesion.

The application of *gyae ma ne nka*, driven by a deliberative system, reveals a number of key elements. First, the element of *listening* to the other. Deliberation involves listening as much as it involves voicing. When we listen, we hear and appreciate the lived experiences of others. It is not a call to change one's mind or to agree with the other. It is to fully engage the other. The Zulu greeting, *sawubona,* is instructive here. It translates as "I see you". The response to the greeting is *yebo, sawubona,* meaning, "I see you seeing me". In other words, I acknowledge you as you acknowledge me. It is a healthy reciprocity. When we see and hear each other by listening and voicing, we give permission to the other to bring all of who they are and embody into a conversation, because these help to demonstrate what we hold valuable. Without the space to hear and listen, we not only appear dismissive, but we fail to gauge the extent to which the issue affects people. While it is good for our mental health to "let it go" at some point, people may need space to process the issue. This way, in cases such as the battered women or the racially charged exchange cited above, people would not feel silenced, shut down, disrespected, or sense discrimination. When *gyae ma ne nka* is invoked, those being advised to let go most likely would have gained more from the conversation than a dismissal.

3.7 Conclusion

Deliberation allows people to weigh various options towards solving a problem, consider the drawbacks and trade-offs, enabling people to determine the options they find appealing and therefore may be willing to support. It provides a healthy space to apply *gyae ma ne nka*. The deliberative framework allows the person offended to process what they hold valuable. These are not instant opinions, neither are they imposed by unfair cultural imperatives. In Christian contexts, the parties can develop options for resolution that are underpinned by Christian texts, and collectively decided.

A deliberative process would not enforce a hasty or unjust *gyae ma ne nka*. On the contrary, the process enables listening to all parties and allows participants to see the implications of such processes including those related to national issues of justice, peace, and stability. Deliberative practices as outlined above reduces the "inhibitors" of *gyae ma ne nka*, such as non-principled hierarchy and exploitative power relations. If *gyae ma ne nka* is applied with the principles of deliberative democratic practices which advance the notion of collective and collaborative work, the chances of excluding segments of society such as women, youth, or those whose sexual orientation is marginalised, will be minimised. It will enhance the inclusivity and cooperative development stipulated by the SDGs. Such an inclusive process will appeal to both the offended and offender and seek to reintegrate community members for the development of the whole as advanced in *Ubuntu*. For religious institutions, deliberative processes act as spaces to address the needs of those who look to religious institutions for leadership, guidance, and compassion. Such approaches also present the institutions as co-creators in the realisation of the SDGs. It places them in a better stance to challenge governments and speak authoritatively on issues of national development, justice, and peace.

References

Aldridge, Alan. (2000). *Religion in the Contemporary World: A Sociological Introduction*. Malden, MA: Polity Press.

Benhabib, Seyla. (December 1994). "Deliberative Rationality and Models of Democratic Legitimacy", *Constellations*, 1(1): 26–52. doi.org/10.1111/j.1467-8675.1994.tb00003.x.

Bewaji, John, and Ramose, Mogobe. (2003). "The Bewaji, Van Binsbergen and Ramose Debate on *Ubuntu*", *South African Journal of Philosophy*, 22(4), 378–415. doi:10.4314/sajpem.v22i4.31380.

Brooks, Cornell. (October 2, 2019). Twitter, https://twitter.com/cornellwbrooks/status/1179534728107626497.

Clements, Keith. (1995). *Learning to Speak: The Church's Voice in Public Affairs*. Edinburgh: T&T Clark.

De Gruchy, John. (2002). *Reconciliation, Restoring Justice*. Minneapolis, MN: Fortress Press, 2002.

Dwamena-Aboagye, Angela. (2021). *Ministering to the Hurting: Women's Mental Health and Pastoral Response in Ghana*. Accra: University of Ghana Press.

Dwamena-Aboagye, Angela. (November 18, 2021). Conversation with Ruby Quantson Davis.

Etukumana, Godwin. (2020). "The Reconciliation of Lepers in Luke 5:12–15 and its Implications for Human Dignity: An African Perspective", in Marius Nel, Dion Forster, & Christo Thesnaar (eds.), *Reconciliation, Forgiveness and Violence in Africa: Biblical, Pastoral and*

Ethical Perspectives. Stellenbosch, South Africa: African Sun Media, 33-49.

Forrester, Duncan. (2000). *Truthful Action: Explorations in Practical Theology.* Edinburgh, UK: T&T Clark.

Forster, Dion. (2018). "Translation and a Politics of Forgiveness in South Africa? What Black Christians Believe, and White Christians Do Not Seem to Understand", *Stellenbosch Theological Journal*, 4(2), 77–94. doi. org/10.17570/stj.2018.v4n2.a04.

Forster, Dion. (2019a). "A Social Imagination of Forgiveness", *Journal of Empirical Theology*, 1(32): 70–88. doi.org/doi:10.1163/15709256-12341387.

Forster, Dion. (2019b). *The (Im)Possibility of Forgiveness: An Empirical Intercultural Bible Reading of Matthew 18:15–35.* Stellenbosch, South Africa: African Sun Media.

Forster, Dion. (2020). "Towards an (Im)possible Politics of Forgiveness? Considering the Complexities of Religion, Race and Politics in South Africa", in Marius Nel, Dion Forster, and Christo Thesnaar (eds.), *Reconciliation, Forgiveness and Violence in Africa: Biblical, Pastoral and Ethical Perspectives.* Stellenbosch, South Africa: SunPress, 51–69. doi:10.18820/9781928480532.

Forster, Dion. (September 10, 2021). Conversation with Ruby Quantson Davis.

Gobodo-Madikizela, Pumla. (2002). "Remorse, Forgiveness, and Rehumanization: Stories from South Africa", *Journal of Humanistic Psychology*, 42(1): 7–32. doi: 10.1177/0022167802421002.

Gobodo-Madikizela, Pumla. (2003). *A Human Being Died that Night: Forgiving Apartheid's Chief Killer.* New York: Houghton Mifflin.

Gobodo-Madikizela, Pumla. (2020). "Aesthetics of Memory, Witness to Violence and a Call to Repair", in Kim Wale, Pumla Gobodo-Madikizela, and Jeffrey Prager (eds.), *Post Conflict Hauntings: Transforming Memories of Historical Trauma.* London: Palgrave Macmillan, 122–149.

Gutman, Amy, and Thompson, Dennis. (2004). *Why Deliberative Democracy?* Princeton, NJ: Princeton University Press.

Gyekye, Kwame. (1997). "Person and Community: In Defense of Moderate Communitarianism", in *Tradition and Modernity: Philosophical Reflections on the African Experience.* New York: Oxford University Press.

Habermas, Jürgen. (1979). *Communication and the Evolution of Society,* translated and introduced by Thomas McCarthy. Boston, MA: Beacon Press.

Kayla. (May 2021). Conversation with Ruby Quantson Davis.

Kusmierz, Katrin, and Cochrane, James. (2013). "Public Church and Public Theology is South Africa's Political Transformation", in Christine Lienemann-Perrin and James Cochrane (eds.), *The Church and the*

Public Sphere in Societies in Transition. Pietermaritzburg, Cluster Publications, 49–85.

Mansbridge, Jane. (2012). "Everyday Talk in the Deliberative System", in Derek Barker, Nöelle McAfee, and David McIvor (eds.), *Democratizing Deliberation: A Political Anthology*. Dayton, OH: Kettering Foundation Press, 85–112.

Maris, Cornelis. (2020). "Philosophical Racism and *Ubuntu*: In Dialogue with Mogobe Ramose", *South African Journal of Philosophy*, 39(3): 308–326. https://doi.org/10.1080/02580136.2020.1809124.

Mathews, David. (2014). *The Ecology of Democracy: Finding Ways to Have a Stronger Hand in Shaping Our Future*. Dayton, OH: Kettering Foundation Press.

Oelofsen, Marietjie. (2020). "Listening for the Quiet Violence in the Unspoken", in *Post-Conflict Hauntings*. New York: Palgrave Macmillan, 177-202.

Ostrom, Elinor. (1993). "Covenanting, Co-Producing, and the Good Society", *Newsletter of PEGS*, 3(2): 7–9. www.jstor.org/stable/20710607.

Pobee, John. (1987). "Religion and Politics in Ghana, 1972–1978: Some Case Studies from the Rule of General I. K. Acheampong", *Journal of Religion in Africa*, 17(1): 44–62. https://doi.org/10.2307/1581075.

Ramphele, Mamphela. (2017). *Dreams, Betrayal and Hope*. Cape Town: Penguin Random House South Africa.

Schubert, Benedict. (2013). "The Role of the Churches from Mozambique's Journey from War to Peace", in Christine Lienemann-Perrin and James Cochrane James (eds.), *The Church and the Public Sphere in Societies in Transition*. Pietermaritzburg, Cluster Publications, 91–139.

Scott, James. (1985). *Weapons of the Weak: Everyday Forms of Peasant Resistance*. New Haven, CT: Yale University Press.

HB 184-18 State v. Lakela Sweswe (2018). http://www.veritaszim.net/node/3070.

Stout, Jeffrey. (2004). *Democracy and Tradition*. Princeton, NJ: Princeton University Press.

Thakhathi, Andani, and Netshitangani, Tshilidzi. (2020). "*Ubuntu*-as-Unity: Indigenous African Proverbs as a 'Re-educating' Tool for Embodied Social Cohesion and Sustainable Development", *African Identities*, 18(4): 407–420. doi.org/10.1080/14725843.2020.1776592.

United Nations. (2015). Sustainable Development Goals. Viewed from www.un.org/sustainabledevelopment [Date accessed October 1, 2021].

Yankelovich, Daniel, 1991. *Coming to Public Judgment: Making Democracy Work in a Complex World*. Syracuse: Syracuse University Press.

4
CASE STUDY 3: CHURCH, CHARITY, AND PHILANTHROPY

Deciding Faith-Based Actions Democratically

4.1 Introduction

Religious organisations and groups took in the equivalent of USD$850 billion in 2021 (World Christian Database 2021). From this, they provided a wide range of charitable services and financial support to causes and issues that they care about and would like to influence. Often, these issues relate to one of the United Nations' 17 SDGs, such as addressing poverty and hunger, strengthening democratic institutions and peace work, or improving health and education. In these efforts at charity and philanthropy, however, not enough religious organisations engage in conversations and actions that could tackle the root causes of the problems they seek to address through their outreach and mission programmes. Deliberations and identifying common ground for action to address underlying issues can help build a shared understanding of the issues and provide more comprehensive and sustainable solutions to the challenges of life together. This chapter explores the possibility for deliberation in religious organisations that can lead to more proactive approaches beyond things like food pantries, financial assistance, temporary homeless shelters, and other social outreach

DOI: 10.4324/9781003214250-5

programmes. The chapter looks at the role that deliberative democratic practices can play in helping churches and other religious organisations understand themselves as part of addressing shared concerns, rather than saviours for "others" in need.

4.2 Christian Philanthropy and Charity

Religious organisations across the globe play a central role in philanthropic and charity work, from large international NGOs, such as World Vision International, Lutheran World Relief and Muslim Aid, to food pantries and provision of other social services organised by local churches. This chapter explores the ways that churches and other faith-based organisations acquire and use resources to address challenges such as poverty, democratic deficits, the environment, violence, and other issues highlighted by the United Nations' SDGs.

The financial resources that churches and other faith-based organisations use to address problems locally, regionally, and globally, is staggering. Church income worldwide is estimated to be USD $340 billion, and the income of parachurch organisations and Christian NGOs is around USD$510 billion dollars (World Christian Database 2021). These figures do not account for informal giving by or between members of religious communities, which is presumed to be substantial, but would be difficult and resource-intensive to track globally. The provision of these funds, along with millions of hours of volunteer time, has notable consequences for the ability of people and communities to address shared challenges. Thus, it is important to consider how such resources are used and how they might be used more effectively.

The story of giving by Christians—of time, energy, and financial resources—is mixed. There is both textual and archaeological evidence that people who identified as part of what we would now call the early Christian church understood that their faith required them to give to, and care for, others (Caner 2018; Concannon 2020). Evidence points towards giving not only in terms of financial resources, but also time and effort. For instance, Acts 4 (dated between 70 and 90 CE) documents how followers of Jesus sold their possessions and pooled their resources so that there would not be "needy among them". In the centuries since, the tradition of Christian care for those who are in need or suffering—framed in a range of ways, including charity, solidarity, philanthropy, or mutual aid—has become central to many understandings of Christian practice (Lynn 2021). Yet, there is also a complex history of giving, philanthropy, charity, and "helping" others that has led to overdependence, harm, suffering, and death.

Often, attempts to help interfere with the ability of communities to work together on challenges they are facing, and can contribute to the perception that they are not capable of creative problem-solving or overcoming obstacles without outside intervention (Funiciello 1993; Lupton 2021; McKnight 1989). In some cases, the efforts at providing help are well-intentioned, even if the outcomes are poor and even if the impetus to "help" is grounded in problematic biases or prejudices. Yet, as discussed in earlier chapters, there is also ample evidence that under the guise of "helping" or "saving", Christians with power and resources have caused great harm, often to women, children, Indigenous people, people of colour, sex/gender/sexual minorities, and people who are poor. This is exemplified in the recent horrific and still-emerging accounts of Canadian residential boarding schools run by Christian organisations, where Indigenous children were forced to attend as recently as 1947. The schools required children to be away from their families and their community, sought to erase Indigenous culture and languages, and there was widespread evidence of physical, sexual, and emotional abuse (Mosby and Millions 2021). Mass and unmarked graves of the children who died of abuse, starvation, accidents, and disease are still being uncovered today. Likewise, across the African continent, there is a long and painful history of missionaries who ostracised and sought to dehumanise Africans, particularly but not limited to those who were not interested in converting to Christianity. The ATRs were treated as backward and evil, as opposed to being equal but alternative belief systems (Nkomazana 2016).

It is thus understandable that philanthropy and charity done in the name of religion are often viewed as suspect by people and communities that are the targets of such efforts. One of the central questions of this chapter is how religiously grounded charity, philanthropy, and other efforts to "make things better", can be undertaken such that it does not cause harm, and supports the ability of everyday people to make decisions about their own lives and to address problems together. While we focus primarily on the Christian context, it is our hope that the insights can also be helpful to other religious contexts where charitable work and philanthropy are an important part of the tradition.

Defining Our Terms

Religious organisations approach the problems they believe need to be fixed in a number of ways and use a range of terms to describe these efforts. These terms vary across different contexts and cultures. Additionally, we have found that often when a term is intended to be used in a particular way, the reality on the ground is quite different from how the work is discussed. As we have acknowledged in other parts of this book, language, and the way we use it, has meaningful consequences. Thus, it is important to discuss terminology and language without distracting from lived experiences and empirical evidence.

The term *charity* derives from the Latin noun *caritas*. The original meaning indicated Christian love of fellow human beings, but over time has come to signify giving to those in need, more generally. There have long been criticisms that such giving does not actually help people in the way givers argue that it does and, in fact, can make things worse. In the late-twentieth and early twenty-first centuries, charity has often come to denote giving that doesn't address problems or promote sustainable well-being or freedom, but just provides a temporary and often easier Band-Aid that is inadequate to the problems at hand (Lupton 2012).

Where charity's etymological roots are Latin, *philanthropy* derives from the ancient Greek term *philanthrôpía* (*philos* meaning "-dear, loved, beloved", and *anthropos* meaning "humanity"). In the broadest sense, it has often been understood to mean love of humanity. Paul Vallely does an excellent job of discussing the complex history and variegated meanings of philanthropy in *Philanthropy: From Aristotle to Zuckerberg* (2020). He notes that while philanthropy is often understood today as someone or some organisation that gives away a significant amount of money for a good cause, historically philanthropy has been understood differently:

> Philanthropy from early on encompassed two radically different interpretations. For the Greeks, and then the Romans, it was about the relationship of the individual to society, and it was bound up with notions of status, honour, and approval. For the Jews, and later Muslims, it was about the relationship of the individual to God—a relationship mediated through a sense of community with fellow believers. Out of a synthesis of these two visions emerged the Christian conception of philanthropy which was to shape ideas of charity and giving for thousands of years of Christendom. This was then tempered by the Reformation and subsequently the enlightenment (19).

In this book, we focus on more contemporary understandings of charity and philanthropy, but it is helpful to know that their meanings have shifted over time, have been contested over time, and continue to shift and be contested today. This chapter is, in some ways, an effort to contribute to the ongoing negotiation about the role of charity and philanthropy, arguing that they have their place as parts of a healthy ecology of democracy which includes faithful people and communities. But, we argue that, as often practised, they are an inadequate response to the challenges people face. There is nothing wrong with charity or philanthropy per se. If your neighbour's house is ruined by a natural disaster, providing them with food, clothing, and shelter while they rebuild and regroup is a reasonable and helpful response. Likewise, if someone makes more money than they need or want to spend on their own life, giving away this money for the good of others is not inherently problematic. In this chapter, we highlight that charity and philanthropy are too often seen as the primary tools that Christians have, to respond to need, to suffering, and to their perception that the world is not as it should be. While these are often easier responses, or those that make us feel good, right, and perhaps righteous, there are rich theological resources and promising examples that point to a more democratic, deliberative, and cooperative approach to addressing needs, suffering, and shared challenges.

4.3 The Saviour Complex: Christian Groups as Givers and Recipients of Aid

With few exceptions, Christian churches and, often, broader denominational structures and parachurch organisations, provide some sort of service to communities where they are located, and many serve in other communities as well (Wuthnow 2014). This can take a programmatic form such as job training, after-school programmes, support groups, or counselling. It also takes the form of emergency response, refugee resettlement, and medical care. Services also involve material help such as cash assistance or free food (Poppendieck 1999). The reasons for service vary and can range from the intention of converting people to Christianity to a commitment to helping people become more self-sufficient and relieving suffering (Corbett and Fikkert 2014; Ellerman 2006; Poppendieck 1999).

Despite important resources in the Christian tradition that emphasise community and joint decision-making, efforts at addressing problems, such as poverty, abuse, environmental degradation, or violence, are rarely framed in terms of building community or strengthening civic capacity. Success stories of individuals who have overcome challenges, such as poverty, addiction, or abuse, abound. Likewise, there are many examples of service activities that have transformed individuals and the organisations that provide those services. However, it is the exception to find accounts of communities where the social services and financial support provided by churches or religious institutions have formed a foundation for people to change the circumstances that led to the problems in the first place. As Reverend Mike Mather noted when discussing his church's food pantry, "Year after year we were still handing out food yet people were still hungry. We felt so good about it that I broke my arm patting myself on the back. But nothing really was actually better" (Mather 2016). In arguing against church social service provision, John McKnight (1989), director of the Asset-Based Community Development Institute, noted, "I have never seen service systems that brought people to well-being, delivered them to citizenship, or made them free" (38).

This section describes the saviour complex and how it contributes to the perpetuation of models of service, philanthropy, and charity that fail to acknowledge, engage, or emphasise the agency, power, and abilities of all people and communities. As touched on throughout our study, biases about who is capable of problem-solving and who is "needy" are at play; dynamics about who has the means to help and who deserves the help of those with means are brought to the fore. Charity, service, and philanthropy allow those with money and free time not only to feel good about helping the "needy", but it also allows them to wield power over "needy" people and their communities. Jordan Flannery touches on this in his chapter, "The History of Saviors" (2016: 25), where he points out that,

> when food, housing and other basic needs become a gift… they are subject to all the prejudices of the generous. The gift can be taken back from those who are not deserving or grateful enough. Those who are too decadent or perverse or lazy or rebellious may not qualify to receive the gift in the first place.

The saviour complex is discussed in psychological literature as a pathology or a literal delusion. But here, we use it more generally to refer to the history and current reality of Christian efforts to "save" people both in an eschatological sense and in a material sense. We discuss why the saviour complex, in its dizzying array of manifestations, continues to hold such great appeal, even as it fails to produce meaningful change and undermines important threads of Christian theology that point towards more democratic and just communities.

One in Christ?

We begin by noting one of the major theological problems with the saviour complex: the extent to which it undercuts Christian ideals of equality and unity highlighted in, among other places, Paul's well-known baptismal formula in Galatians 3:28:

> There is no longer Jew or Greek, there is no longer slave or free, there is no longer male and female; for all of you are one in Christ Jesus.

The saviour complex necessarily ranks those with means—money, resources, time, health, privilege—over those who need "saving" of one sort or another. Here, theologian Elisabeth Schüssler Fiorenza's concept of the "kyriarchal pyramid" is helpful. Kyriachy is a neologism she created from the Greek words *kyrios* "lord, master" and Greek *archè*, "authority, domination, sovereignty" to highlight that there are "intersecting structures of domination... ruling and oppression" (Schüssler Fiorenza 2001: 211).

The kyriarchal pyramid can be used to describe the world in which we live (and have long lived), where certain groups of people not only have more power and enjoy more freedom, but they either seek to maintain this system, or at least fail to work to dismantle the system that unjustly favours them. Within this pyramid, one dynamic is those who are "saviours" and those who "need saving". This dynamic has developed in countless ways across time and place: races that need "saving", genders that need "saving", the poor, widowed, orphaned, homeless, hungry, immigrants, and children … the list of those imagined to be in need of saving by others is long. While it is clear there are many efforts at "saving" that revel in domination and ruling, even many well-intentioned efforts at service, charity, and philanthropy that are sincere responses to religious conviction that reinforce divisions and hierarchy among God's people. Here, we are reminded of the statement from Saint Bernard of Clairvaux, a mediaeval Christian monk and mystic:

> *L'enfer est plein de bonnes volontés ou désirs.*
> The road to hell is paved with good wishes and desires.

Saint Bernard himself is an excellent example of this: in his presumably "good wishes" to promote the Christian faith, he was an advocate of the Christian Crusades that resulted in the forcible conversion and tragic deaths of millions.

Whether one has been the giver of "help" or the recipient of it, it is easy to observe that such dynamics reinforce that some people have the unearned privilege to name and frame the issues, make the rules, solve the problems, and control the narrative, while others do not. Such situations are eloquently addressed in the pioneering work of Brazilian educator and critical theorist Paulo Freire who noted, "Any situation in which some [people] prevent others from engaging in the process of inquiry is one of violence… to alienate humans from their own decision-making is to change them into objects" (1970: 70). How might Christian practices instead acknowledge and affirm the full humanity and subjectivity of all people?

To reject the saviour complex is to affirm that all of God's people have the ability to hear God's voice, to learn together, and to act together. This does not ignore current power imbalances or structural explanations for suffering or need, but rather highlights that in order to undermine such imbalances and structures we must begin by naming all people as full participants in the soteriological universe.

The Hard Work of Real Change Together

Even though there is little evidence that more charity or social services, in and of themselves, transforms the ways that citizens and communities function, the saviour complex maintains its appeal in part because it involves clear action that everyday people can take. This approach is often not taxing for volunteers or church members, does not threaten power structures, and feels very rewarding, which means that significant numbers of people are able and willing to participate in such efforts. While there are Christian leaders and movements which suggest that living as a Christian should result in radical sacrifice (e.g. Claiborne 2006), the reality is that most churches rely on those who have jobs, families, economic pressures, and a disinclination towards more sacrificial modes of religiosity (Bowler 2013).

For many, charity and philanthropy are an achievable and important way that people and churches attempt to address the problems they see in their communities, and the services they provide, in fact, meet urgent and real needs in communities. As one volunteer said,

> I wish there was a way to change the fact that people are hungry and struggling and I hope that gets figured out, but I don't know how to do that. I do know how to volunteer at the food pantry.
>
> *Anonymous Interview (2019)*

This highlights the way that the volunteer sees herself helping other people who are hungry, as if hunger is the problem of the hungry and not a more fundamental problem of the society she is living in. When we are able to shift from viewing problems as "other people's problems" that we are "helping with" and rather as our own problems that we, as a collective, have created together, we may be able to begin a transition into cooperative problem-solving that addresses challenges of life together.

Measuring Salvation

While the issues with the saviour complex could occupy the whole chapter (or entire book) the final issue we will touch on here is the allure of creating social service, charity, and philanthropy programmes where the leaders can easily track the outcomes: how many meals were served, how many people accepted Jesus, how many beds were filled, and how much money was spent. When social services and charity produce measurable outcomes, churches and organisations can report back to donors how money was spent and can show future donors all the good that was done. If an organisation figures out how to do what they do very well (e.g., 90 percent of graduates go on to college; 85 percent of addicts stay in recovery for a year) they can expand their programmes, get more money, and "save" more people. Yet, replication of "best practices" and "good programmes" often leaves out the creative learning that comes from everyday people working together to talk about, make sense of, and act together on the roots of their shared challenges (Frederickson 2003). "Good programmes" often do not leave room for productive failure or struggle, which often stifles the learning and change that are essential for citizens to collaboratively address problems.

In conversations among clergy about this aspect of the saviour complex, many also noted that efficient and "successful" programmes can crowd out space for congregations, members, and the community to experience and connect both with God and with each other. "There is a risk", one senior pastor notes, "that these become motions to go through". It is clear that some churches get so invested in predictable programmes with "good outcomes" where many people are "saved" (from homelessness, hunger, illness, abuse, addiction... the list goes on) that continuing the successful model becomes the goal, rather than addressing the underlying issues that might lead to the need for such programmes in the first place. They lose sight of the risky, messy, and radical work of the church which has strong historical and theological roots in Christian tradition and scripture, in favour of predictability and manageability of reproducible and scalable programmes (Mather 2018).

In this chapter we explore what it can look like when churches, faith communities, and NGOs use a deliberative approach to address the issues that they are concerned about, and to gain a deeper understanding about the problems they see and experience.

4.4 The Money and the Conversation: Learning from the COVID-19 Pandemic and Christian Philanthropic Efforts

COVID-19 has highlighted the inequities that exist in society. In the United States, African American communities and other minority and marginalised groups have been more impacted by the pandemic than any other racial group (Winston 2021; Jones and DeMott 2021). Countries like Ghana, South Africa, and Zimbabwe have struggled to manage hospitalisation related to COVID-19, and vaccination efforts in the Global South have been severely limited because of restricted access to adequate doses of vaccine. For some individuals, the church may be the only formal institution they are affiliated with. Has the church been, and could the church be, a place of refuge in a pandemic, to provide and to care for the vulnerable while also working to increase community capacity to address challenges in the future?

In many parts of Africa where the church is very vibrant, COVID-19 restrictions meant closure of churches. It also caused a reduction in income, as many churches thrive on tithes and offerings given in-person during church services. Unlike the Global North, where electronic transactions are widely employed in all aspects of life (including church offerings), in most churches in Africa, the physical collection of money is the way that offertory is made to the church. Some churches, particularly in the United States, promptly pivoted to online services and reached out to people virtually. However, this was not the case in most countries. The ability to worship and meet online was dependent on a number of factors, including the demographics of the congregation, the use of technology prior to the pandemic, and the availability of technology. Over time, socially distanced worship services started slowly; however, with decreased capacity, church incomes dwindled.

Churches in Africa and elsewhere faced their own existential threats, revealing their fragility. While some churches could reach out to global partners, churches everywhere were themselves deeply affected by the pandemic: their already low numbers of congregants were further reduced. In places like the United Kingdom, some churches that provide support for partner churches in the Global South also faced permanent closure, with the need to sell church buildings as maintenance became a struggle. This also surfaced the dependence syndrome that is often associated with traditional aid.

It is worth noting however, that during times of the most intense pandemic crisis, many philanthropic groups, including Christian groups and individuals, became conduits for channelling support to where it was needed. In many places, ordinary citizens acted in small ways to support one another. Mutual aid efforts have seen significant growth in the pandemic times, highlighting the interdependence of those who can give and those who are in need at the moment. In many mutual aid contexts, those who can give do, and those who are in need receive, but the gatekeeping and dehumanising aspects of traditional aid are not present. There is no need to "prove" who is in need or what they will do with the funds given in the context of mutual aid. You are in need: I give. I am in need: I ask. We trust each other in the context of a vision where everyday people work together to create the world that we all want to live in.

A report by the SIVIO Institute, "The Best of Us in the Worst of Times, A Review of the Coronavirus Pandemic: COVID-19 and Philanthropic Responses", (Jowah et al. 2021) captures the ambivalence that is woven throughout the pandemic crisis:

> the pandemic has probably brought the worst out of most of our leaders and the best out of the ordinary citizens (3).

The report chronicles a number of citizen-led initiatives in response to community needs during the pandemic. People quickly mobilise to address issues together, even in the face of institutional red tape. Religious institutions have an important role to play in helping members and those in surrounding communities develop the "feel for the game" (as per Bourdieu) of responding to needs in ways that allow for naming, framing, deliberation, and acting grounded in the lived experiences of those who are impacted by challenges.

Crisis creates opportunity, and the pandemic has created the space for innovative responses. Although fraught with much confusion, the pandemic offered an opportunity to reframe congregational engagement, restructure decision-making processes, and create the environment for people to develop a culture of responding to needs in ways that contribute to a sustainable development agenda in their localities and countries.

At the centre of these issues are questions of power. The church as an institution is also a centre of power and a machinery that determines where resources go and who benefits from such resources. For the purposes of our argument here, we also submit that, given the power it wields, the church is well-placed to change actions around "giving", charity, or philanthropy in ways that support transparency and multidimensional accountability, and enable recipients of such giving to transition into empowered civic actors.

A Deliberative and Democratic Approach to Philanthropy and Charity

How can religious groups engage communities in transformational ways? Whose concerns are religious groups addressing? How were those concerns identified, discussed, and resolved?

These questions get to the issue of what a deliberative approach to philanthropy and charity might look like. Within the scope of inclusive governance and global peace and stability, how the church engages the "needy" matters. An important step will be discussions between those typically understood as the givers and those traditionally understood as in-need. The evidence that personal and institutional transformation can occur in the wake of well-thought-out engagement across difference is substantial (Saunders 2011). Increasingly, it is becoming clear that simply providing goods and services and dumping pre-loved items may not be enough.

One way of moving forward is to enable people to be part of decisions that pertain to their well-being and development. A key deliberative practice here is issue identification and concern-gathering. People's lives will not be transformed unless all of those involved, "givers" and "receivers", come together to reframe the issue such that it is everyone's problem, not just the people traditionally understood to be "in need." People often know the best way to address the problem based on their lived experiences. Essentially, working and struggling together to arrive at these answers is formative and essential. We can only learn to act together and address our challenges together if we are allowed to develop the skills and civic muscle to do so. Part of this is naming and framing the issue together, acting on the issue together, and then learning from the process particularly when it does not turn out exactly how we envisioned or hoped. This process is less about dictating what help others get, and more about building lasting skills by which people can address pressing issues in their communities.

A deliberative approach to philanthropy and charity will require people to be willing to give up the power and the privilege that they enjoy as people who have more, and giving up our deeply held beliefs that we know more than others about their own lives and experiences. One reason why philanthropy does not tackle the root causes of issues is that sometimes those who have power and privilege are quite content to send money, cans of soup, and already-used items they don't need. This is much easier than engaging in the hard talk of policy change, even though many are in positions to do so at various levels.

It is worth noting, however, that in places like Africa, the church is for the most part also a recipient of aid, either from its local congregations or overseas partners. If the church uses such resources on its establishment rather than build a transformative philanthropic system, the dependence on aid will continue. The COVID-19 pandemic has made visible the vulnerability of church institutions and their congregations, especially where external help is curtailed.

How can the traditional recipients of philanthropy make progress to becoming subjects (as per Paulo Freire) rather than objects in the philanthropic universe? Such a "power shift" will require a change in the "saviour or messianic posture of givers" to a place where we ask the difficult and oft ignored questions. We acknowledge the extraordinary complexity of a dynamic where those who have been traditionally marginalised and discriminated against, are also those who must in some ways push back on the saviour mindset of those from whom they wish to obtain resources. There are no easy answers here. We call on the traditional "givers" to challenge themselves, their colleagues, and partners to do whatever is possible to remove the burden of changing the philanthropic system from those who are already disadvantaged by the philanthropic system. This will require uncomfortable and meaningful steps towards relinquishing power.

For readers that are in the "giving" position, the first step is to acknowledge the dynamic at hand and work towards a psychological openness to saying, "We do not know best". It is hard to give up power, even if we imagine we wield it with the best intentions. Even the philanthropist with the best intentions still benefits from and acts in a system woven through with injustice, inequity, and unearned privilege. Traditional "givers" can ask themselves:

- Who are the recipients? Do we know them, "see" them, or are they just people in some distant land?
- Is the problem framed by the givers, or by those impacted by the issue?
- Are recipients involved in the decision-making machinery?
- If they are, what is motivating them to be "in the room"?
- What are the insights they bring?
- How do they inform giving?
- Is there an alignment between what givers offer and what recipients need?
- Does giving, charity, and philanthropy empower?

In sum, who is making decisions around philanthropy and how do such actions impact lives sustainably? To make progress on addressing these challenges, democratic practices such as naming, framing, deliberating, acting together, and learning together are essential. These are iterative processes. As we have discussed, they require all involved being willing to trust people to make decisions about their lives, to allow people to fail as they try to address challenges so that they might learn, and to let go of a fixation on measuring and counting as the primary measure of "success."

4.5 Nurturing Global Philanthropy in the Church through Democratic Practices

The problems discussed above call for a change in approaches and mindset towards resource mobilisation. First, the "messianic" or saviour mindset both within local churches and among global partners needs rethinking. Second, heads of church institutions ought to rethink the sources and use of resources.

Building on What Exists

While the word *philanthropy* may not be used, the notion of giving has long been part of African culture. In a webinar on "Giving in Zimbabwe", convened in October 2021 by the SIVIO Institute in Harare, the Director of the Centre on African Philanthropy and Social Investment observed "we are born philanthropists and grow to become beneficiaries of philanthropy". There has always been individual giving, often to support relatives, friends, and colleagues. Over the lifetime of most Africans, there is a flow of aid, resources, and help through cash or in-kind, goods or services. These range from clothing, equipment, land, building, money, and food to skills and knowledge. "Loaning" is also a form of giving. In some parts of Africa, it is not unusual to see a rich man "loan" a cow to a poor family or someone in crisis for a period of time. During this period, the cow grazes the land, provides milk for meals and manure for farming, which enhances livelihood and provides prestige and dignity. The capacity to quickly mobilise and respond to needs and crises is incredible. Funerals provide particular insights in various parts of Africa. For example, in Zimbabwe, it is customary to give the bereaved family money, referred to as *chema*, which translates as "crying, we are crying with you". The money is to assist with funeral expenses, with the understanding that "no one buries alone". We invite readers to reflect on the ways that similar practices are part of their own cultures, religious practices, and community habits.

As we wrote this chapter, we recognised the many ways we and our families and friends have experienced philanthropy. We have included several of our own accounts here as a way to highlight the centrality of lived experiences in understanding, navigating, and ultimately changing the predominant models of charity and philanthropy. This is not only what we do in our careers, or via institutions, but the reshaping of our *habitus* through practices is part

Case Study 3: Church, Charity, and Philanthropy

of everyday life. In naming this and building on this, we encounter ways to transform our own lives and the lives and institutions to which we are connected.

Co-author Elizabeth Gish recalls her experiences of the complexity of engaging in charity and philanthropy in her teen years:

> Growing up in a lower-middle class family in a farming community, I was aware of the poverty that my family struggled with, yet basic needs were always met and I had a relatively protected existence as a child, attending a nearly all-White rural school. Serious problems such as violence, hunger, and homelessness were mostly on the news and not in my daily life. To the extent that they impacted those in my community, they were often hidden and considered private. When my primarily White large church in the midwestern United States exposed me to building houses for those struggling with shelter, travelling to other countries on "service" trips, volunteering at orphanages, tutoring at underfunded schools, and summer programmes for children, I felt good about helping people in need. However, over time, through mentors and reading books such as Jonathan Kozol's *Amazing Grace* (2005), I questioned my efforts and those of my church. I was praised for my work, and got scholarships to college for "service", but the people in the neighbourhoods where I volunteered still went to underresourced schools, still struggled to make a living wage, still struggled to get enough food on their table, and still faced police discrimination and violence that I did not have to worry about in my community. Year after year, the church spent lots of resources on volunteer programmes and trips abroad, yet conditions in these communities remained mostly the same. When the children aged out of the "programmes", they were all but forgotten. I came to understand that the very practices that felt important and helpful to me to grow and learn about a life beyond my protected existence were also perpetuating inequality and injustice, and reinforced problematic notions about who is the subject

and who is the object; about who is capable of taking part in their own growth, healing, and liberation.

Gish's experiences highlight the double-edged sword of volunteerism and charity: on the one hand, her engagement in "service" allowed her to learn first-hand about issues of injustice and inequality and ultimately to question the systems that created the need for such service; on the other hand, she benefited from her service via scholarships and accolades far more than those whom she "served". How do we create workable paths of engagement across differences while transforming problematic structures that undermine equality, mercy, and justice and perpetuate racial, ethnic, gendered, and class stereotypes?

Co-author Kudakwashe Chitsike experienced a typical African philanthropic response as this chapter developed:

> When my sister narrated a predicament of her childminder, my immediate response was, let's appeal to our friends in the various groups to which we belong. The baby-minder, a widow, leaves her four children in the care of her mother while she works. Her ten-year-old daughter was cooking in the morning with hot oil and the pan caught fire. She didn't realise that the flames hit the thatched roof of the rural kitchen. She only put out the fire on the pan and left for school. The whole kitchen and its contents caught fire and burnt to the ground. No one was able to put the fire out. The ten-year-old and her seven-year-old brother sleep in the kitchen so their blankets were also burnt. As the sole breadwinner, the baby-minder was distraught; it is up to her to rebuild the kitchen and replace everything. My sister appealed to a small group of friends and we immediately committed to re-stocking the kitchen and ensuring that the children have blankets within the week. It was easy for us to respond quickly and provide exactly what was needed, as this had been specified in the request. Recognising that we had more than enough in our own kitchens, we were motivated to help. We also acknowledged and appreciated the assistance

that the baby-minder provides. She is away from her own children helping to raise my nephew, and to earn money for her family. These sentiments are deeply rooted in our cultural and religious upbringing. In a later conversation I found out that the church the family attends bought the children beds, something they didn't have before. What started off as an awful situation ended on a positive note.

This experience raises greater questions. What are the sustainable avenues for a widow in this situation towards poverty reduction and shelter? What other roles can the church have? Can group efforts encourage tackling some of the root causes of this situation to mitigate inequality?

Co-author Ruby Quantson Davis shares the charitable efforts of alumni associations in Ghana:

> Old student unions or associations have gone beyond networking, maintaining school friendship to significant contributions to their alma mater while supporting members. I highlight here, in particular, high (secondary) school associations. These have become co-providers. Heads of schools regularly engage leaders or executives of these associations presenting a list of needs in the school. Such needs would range from a school bus to buildings and textbooks. Alumni groups often operate as year groups (for example, "class of 1991"). This means each group takes on a project to support the school. The alumni year group I belong to recently decided to provide the school with a water storage facility or tank. The relevant professionals in the group travelled to the school to assess the feasibility of the project and presented a budget which generated a quota for each member to pay over a few months and to raise funds from among family and friends. At the time of writing this, the initial GH₵50,000 (about USD$7,500) target had been exceeded by nearly a hundred percent. The water tank was presented by members of the year group in a homecoming ceremony. It was a joyful day.

The notion of alumni helping the alma mater is not new. Often, however, it is rich individuals who contribute to the endowment. In a place like Ghana, there is no such "discrimination". The reasons behind such efforts are multiple. A key element is that there is a sense of giving inculcated into children and students, particularly as religion is highly present in nearly all schools. This notion of giving is connected to the fact that the school has given to us (knowledge and life skills), and it is time to give back. Simple reciprocity. Is this encouraging dependence and an absence of a sustainable business plan for schools? Is there room for the professional skills to be mobilised to advance a change in policy that enables schools to flourish? Are religious schools like this one able or willing to go beyond occasional giving to transformative actions?

In 2013, the African Philanthropy Network mapped out four types of philanthropic activities conducted by individuals, organisations, and communities (African Grantmakers Network). These were in-kind and service philanthropy, mobilised philanthropy, community-based philanthropy and high net worth and institutional philanthropy. In recent times, conversations around African philanthropy have increased in an attempt to shift the power around development aid.

Giving, in all forms, could be strengthened if the act is perceived as part of a response to local, national, and global socioeconomic challenges. Such giving also ought to be cognisant of the power structures that could be perpetuated through giving. Over time, it needs to transform the lives of recipients, enable them to transition from a state of need and empower recipients to take actions that improve their communities. These are by no means easy actions and the space and infrastructure for pursuing such advocacy may be too daunting for poorer communities and individuals or simply unavailable in certain places. Yet, in places where the church is a major presence in the lives of people and their communities, the power that the church wields as an institution could play an instrumental role in restructuring giving. These could be done in a number of ways including: (1) approaching charity as a development contribution and enabling congregants to see their roles in that agenda; (2) creating pathways to engage recipients of philanthropic efforts in ways that are transparent and transformative; and (3) enabling recipients and congregants to act to influence policy and address the root causes of the issue charitable giving seeks to address. Unless these find priority in the church's agenda, efforts at giving will address immediate needs but fail to be transformative. Times of crisis—such as the COVID-19 pandemic—will reveal the cracks in giving.

References

Anonymous Food Pantry Volunteer. (July 2019). Interview by Elizabeth Gish, Bowling Green, KY.

African Grantmakers Network. (2013), "Sizing the Field: Framework for a New Narrative of African Philanthropy". Viewed from https://africanphilanthropy.issuelab.org/resources/15190/15190.pdf [Date Accessed August 14, 2022].

Bowler, Kate. (2013). *Blessed: A History of the American Prosperity Gospel.* New York: Oxford University Press.

Caner, Daniel. (2018). "Clemency, A Neglected Aspect of Early Christian Philanthropy", *Religions*, 9(8). doi.org/10.3390/rel9080229.

Claiborne, Shane. (2006). *The Irresistible Revolution: Living as an Ordinary Radical.* Grand Rapids, MI: Zondervan.

Concannon, Cavan. (March 30, 2020). "What Early Christian Communities Tell Us about Giving Financial Aid at a Time of Crisis", *The Conversation*. Viewed from https://theconversation.com/what-early-christian-communities-tell-us-about-giving-financial-aid-at-a-time-of-crises-134730 [Date accessed October 15, 2021].

Corbett, Steve, and Fikkert, Brian. (2014). *When Helping Hurts: How to Alleviate Poverty without Hurting the Poor... and Yourself.* Chicago: Moody Publishers.

Dubnick, Melvin, and Frederickson, George. (2011). *Public Accountability: Performance Measurement, the Extended State, and the Search for Trust.* Dayton, OH: Kettering Foundation. Viewed from http://papers.ssrn.com/sol3/papers.cfm?abstract_id=1875024 [Date accessed September 20, 2021].

Ellerman, David. (2006). "Good Intentions: The Dilemma of Outside-In for Inside-Out Change", *Nonprofit Quarterly*, 13(3): 46–49. Viewed from https://nonprofitquarterly.org/2006/09/21/good-intentions-the-dilemma-of-outside-in-help-for-inside-out-change/ [Date accessed October 21, 2021].

Ernst, Manfred. (2012). "Changing Christianity in Oceania: A Regional Overview". *Archives de Sciences Sociales des Religions*, 157: 29–45. doi.org/10.4000/assr.23613.

Flaherty, Jordan. (2016). *No More Heroes: Grassroots Challenges to the Savior Mentality*. Chico, CA: AK Press.

Frederickson, H. George. (2003). *Easy Innovation and the Iron Cage: Best Practice, Benchmarking, Ranking, and the Management of Organizational Creativity. An Occasional Paper of the Kettering Foundation*. Dayton, OH. Viewed from www.kettering.org/catalog/product/easy-innovation-and-iron-cage-best-practice-benchmarking-ranking-and-management [Date accessed October 21, 2021].

Freire, Paulo. (1970). *Pedagogy of the Oppressed*. New York: Herder and Herder.

Funiciello, Theresa. (1993). *Tyranny of Kindness: Dismantling the Welfare System to End Poverty in America*. New York: Atlantic Monthly Press.

Horrell, Dana. (2019). *Engage! Tools for Ministry in the Community*. Minneapolis, MN: Fortress Press.

Human Rights Watch. (April 25, 2019). "Mozambique: Cyclone Victims Forced to Trade Sex for Food". Viewed from www.hrw.org/news/2019/04/25/mozambique-cyclone-victims-forced-trade-sex-food [Date accessed November 8, 2021].

Johnson, Todd, and Zurlo, Gina (eds.). (2021). *World Christian Database*. Leiden/Boston: Brill. www.worldchristiandatabase.org.

Jones, Tracie Denise, and DeMott, Sarah. (November 21, 2021). "A Guide to Black American Experiences During COVID-19." Cambridge, MA: Harvard University Library. Viewed from https://guides.library.harvard.edu/BlackCovid [Date accessed January 10, 2022].

Jowah, Eddah, Garwe, Sandra, and Satuku, Shelly. (February 2021). "The Best of Us in the Worst of Times, A Review of Giving During the Corona Virus Pandemic COVID-19 and Philanthropic Responses". Harare, Zimbabwe: SIVIO Institute.

Kozol, Jonathan. (2005). *Amazing Grace: The Lives of Children and the Conscience of a Nation*. New York: Crown.

Lupton, Robert. (2012). *Toxic Charity: How Churches and Charities Hurt Those They Help (and How to Reverse It)*. New York: HarperOne.

Lutheran World Federation. (March 20, 2019). "Churches in Southern Africa Respond to Devastation: Cyclone Idai". Viewed from https://www.lutheranworld.org/news/churches-southern-africa-respond-devastation-cyclone-idai [Date accessed November 9, 2021].

Lynn, Monty. (2021). *Christian Compassion: A Charitable History*. Portland, OR: Wipf & Stock.

Mather, Michael. (May 2016). Phone conversation with Elizabeth Gish.

Mather, Michael. (2018). *Having Nothing, Possessing Everything: Finding Abundant Community in Unexpected Places*. Grand Rapids, MI: Eerdmans.

Mathews, David. (2002). *For Communities to Work*. Dayton, OH: Kettering Foundation. Viewed from www.kettering.org/catalog/product/communities-work [Date accessed October 12, 2021].

Matsa, Mark, and Dzawanda, Beauty. (June 2014). "Dependency Syndrome by Communities or Insufficient Ingestion Period by Benefactor Organizations? The Chirumanzu Caritas Community Gardening Project Experience in Zimbabwe", *Journal of Geography and Earth Sciences*, 2 (1): 127–148. http://jgesnet.com/journals/jges/Vol_2_No_1_June_2014/7.pdf.

McKnight, John. (Jan/Feb 1989). "Why Servanthood is Bad", *The Other Side*: 33–40. Viewed from https://mn.gov/mnddc/mcKnight/documents/Why_Servanthood_is_Bad.pdf [Date accessed September 19, 2021].

Mosby, Ian, and Millions, Erin. (2021). "Canada's Residential Schools Were a Horror", *Scientific American*, August 1, 2021. Viewed from www.scientificamerican.com/article/canadas-residential-schools-were-a-horror/ [Date accessed November 1, 2021].

Nkomazana, Fidelis, and Setume, Senzokuhle. (2016). "Missionary Colonial Mentality and the Expansion of Christianity in Bechuanaland Protectorate, 1800 to 1900", *Journal for the Study of Religion*, 29(2): 29–55. www.jstor.org/stable/24902913.

Pellowe, John. (2020). "Religion and Philanthropy: How Does a Place of Worship Really Benefit the Public?" *Philanthropist Journal*, July 15, 2020. Viewed from https://thephilanthropist.ca/2020/07/religion-and-philanthropy-how-does-a-place-of-worship-really-benefit-the-public/ [Date accessed October 24, 2021].

Pierce, Gregory F. Augustine. (1984). *Activism that Makes Sense: Congregations and Community Organisation*. Chicago: ACTA Publications.

Pillay, Jerry. (2017). "The Church as a Transformation and Change Agent", *HTS Teologiese Studies/Theological Studies*, 73(3). doi.org/10.4102/hts.v73i3.4352

Poppendieck, Janet. (1999). *Sweet Charity? Emergency Food and the End of Entitlement*. New York: Penguin.

Schüssler Fiorenza, Elisabeth. (2001). *Wisdom Ways: Introducing Feminist Biblical Interpretation*. Maryknoll, NY: Orbis Books.

Saunders, Hal. (2011). *Sustained Dialogue in Conflicts: Transformation and Change*. New York: Palgrave Macmillan.

Taub, Amanda. (2020). "A New Covid Crisis: Domestic Abuse Rises Worldwide", *New York Times*, April 6, 2020. Viewed from www.nytimes.com/2020/04/06/world/coronavirus-domestic-violence.html [Date accessed November 9, 2021].

Vallely, Paul. (2020). *Philanthropy: From Aristotle to Zuckerberg.* London: Bloomsbury Continuum.

Wood, Hannelie. (2019). "Gender Inequality: The Problem of Harmful, Patriarchal, Traditional and Cultural Gender Practices in the Church", *HTS Teologiese Studies/Theological Studies*, 75(1). doi.org/10.4102/hts.v75i1.5177.

Winston, Pamela. (April 2021). "COVID-19 and Economic Opportunity: Unequal Effects on Economic Need and Program Response", Office of the Assistant Secretary for Planning & Evaluation, US Department of Health and Human Services. Viewed from https://aspe.hhs.gov/sites/default/files/migrated_legacy_files//199921/covid-19-human-service-response-brief.pdf [Date accessed January 10, 2022].

Winter, Bruce. (1994). *Seek the Welfare of the City: Christians as Benefactors and Citizens.* Grand Rapids, MI: Eerdmans.

Wuthnow, Robert. (2014). *Saving America? Faith-Based Services and the Future of Civil Society.* Princeton, NJ: Princeton University Press.

5
NOW WHAT? RECOMMENDATIONS AND IMPLICATIONS FOR POLICY MAKERS, RELIGIOUS LEADERS, RESEARCHERS, AND PRACTITIONERS

5.1 Implication One: Redefining Politics to Embrace Everyday Choices

A key reason why religious groups, institutions, and individuals shy away from development discourses is that in most places such activities have been politicised. What this means is that people often say they do not want to engage in "politics". By politics, they mean partisan and institutional politics. Such politics have been associated with divisions and animosity and are bereft of peace. However, if reframed to describe the choice work that citizens have to engage in order to make or influence decisions that affect their well-being, ordinary citizens might be more inclined to engage issues highlighted in the SDGs. Religious spaces, which often attract large gatherings of citizens in the places studied in this book, might be the place to demystify conversations around development and encourage citizen engagement around the United Nations' SDGs.

5.2 Implication Two: The Need for Cross-Fertilisation of Ideas among Religious Groups

There are religious organisations that are at the forefront of deepening the engagement of their members in development processes and communities. Others go beyond charity work to influence development policies through regular conversations on topical issues and experiments in their congregations, as cited in this book. However, because of denominational divides and doctrinal differences, there is often little sharing among religious groups. The increase in ecumenical and interfaith dialogues helps to share ideas, but also needs to address the anxieties some may have in associating with persons of different faiths and beliefs. Often, where there has been the culture of deliberative conversations among church groups, development themes have been more successfully addressed. It is useful for religious leaders to create platforms for such exchanges. Similarly, practitioners and researchers of deliberative democratic practices can make concrete efforts to expose religious groups to useful practices and highlight the places in religious traditions, where democratic and deliberative practices are already part of religious tradition and the life of the religious community. This need not be an outsider activity, as many religious groups have individuals who are practitioners and professionals among them. What is needed are spaces for experimentation, where new ideas and practices can be carried out without the fear of judgement if the efforts are not successful or perfect the first time. Communities must have the space to make mistakes so that they can learn together. When people work on common problems, they find mutual interest and people are better able to recognise their common humanity. This work is not easy, but it is quite possible.

5.3 Implication Three: Intersectoral Collaboration and Learning

Related to the above, is the challenge of cooperation across various sectors. This book has been anchored in SDGs 16 and 17, which emphasise participation and cooperation. To explore the potentials in the interface of religious and democratic practices, the gaps between academia, researchers, civic groups, religious organisations, and policy makers ought to be narrowed. There is much that researchers can learn from cultures where traditional and religious practices are intricately linked to everyday lives. Similarly, communities need opportunities to align their practices with fair and just democratic practices. The outcomes of such interaction should inform policymaking and decision-making on key elements of the SDGs. Given that no single sector can achieve the development goals, such learning ought to be intentional. There are growing examples of intersectoral learning; however, often relevent and on-the-ground groups are often only invited to participate in meetings. It will take more than meetings. Cooperation ought to occur at the inception and conceptualisation stages to help gather insights from various groups. The deliberative practices proposed in this book provide structure and focus for such conversations to generate useful and collective outcomes.

5.4 Implication Four: Build on Local Epistemologies and Traditional Practices

The disconnect between religious practices and democratic practices has often been the result of global knowledge systems that do not incorporate various forms of knowing. In this book, we have attempted to align beneficial democratic and religious practices that help citizens to engage in development processes and improve their lives. To foster greater collaboration, systems of learning, knowledge sources, and various ways of engagement from different parts of the world ought to be surfaced. Religious groups, civil society actors, researchers, and policy makers tend to create such spaces. It is important to ask not just who is missing, but also whose epistemology is downplayed or eliminated. People get disempowered when they are forced to use knowledge systems to which they cannot relate. This must form part of the decolonisation and locally led development agenda and must involve persons who are able to facilitate communications between different knowledge systems to provide the needed bridges and translations.

5.5 Implication Five: Women's Voices in Decision-Making

Women's voices in various spaces, both religious and secular, are still too often silenced, ignored, or excluded. This book particularly highlights sexual violence as a critical area where decisions ought to be informed by women, especially by the stories of victims and survivors. As violence against women is often justified by traditional and religious texts, religious groups have an obligation to do more to change the narratives in their contexts. Heads of religious institutions, committees, groups, and guilds have an essential role to play. Supported by feminist and womanist readings of sacred texts, positive cultural norms, and deliberative spaces as described in this book, religious leaders can provide safer spaces for women to seek support, inform policies, and actively take on empowering roles. In the places cited in this book, where women are often in the majority in congregations, changes in gender narratives within the church can go a long way to influence state and national policies.

5.6 Implication Six: Charities and Policy Influence

This book proposes that charitable activities can take people out of dependence on charities and achieve greater self-sufficiency and sustainability. One approach to this is to involve recipients in the decisions that affect them, and ultimately seek to transform the division between recipients and givers. This gives those who are typically recipients of help the opportunity to name the problem in ways that are meaningful to them. This is enabling and empowering. It also offers givers the opportunity to learn and work collaboratively to achieve the SDGs. As charity is one of the core practices of religious groups, a shift in the way charity is understood and carried out can sustainably improve livelihoods. Conversations with those affected also have the potential to generate not just immediate outputs but also decisions that can provide effective policy alternatives.

5.7 Implication Seven: Theological Appraisal and Training

The interaction between deliberative democratic practices and religion, as described in this book, also surfaces the intricate link between faith and culture (Meyer 2011). In the countries and contexts cited, scriptures have often been interpreted through cultural lenses that are both inhibiting to sections of society such as women, and life-giving in other instances. Sometimes, we carry our cultural baggage into church and embellish it with scriptures, as remarked by theologian and women's advocate Angela Dwamena-Aboagye in a November 2021 conversation with co-author Ruby Quantson Davis. To what extent should the Bible and other religious texts be an interpretive framework for our cultures, or vice-versa, in ways that generate improved practices? This suggests a broader study beyond the scope of this book. However, in the search for answers, a periodic theological appraisal of religious and democratic practices within specific cultural contexts and guided by improved humanitarian frameworks (such as the SDGs), should inform which practices are worth upholding and those that should be modified or discarded. This further requires consistent capacity development for church leaders and workers. Based on the cases discussed in this book, some of the skills-upgrading and knowledge-building required should include: (1) issue identification; (2) framing, creating, and facilitating deliberative spaces; (3) mediation; (4) promoting collective action; (5) mental health support; and (6) leadership. Some denominations have incorporated some of these skills into pastoral supervision. The work of Jane Leach (2007, 2020) on pastoral theology and creative supervision is useful for counsellors, church workers, and other helping professionals. As suggested within the framework of this book, religious groups cannot do this alone. Collaboration with researchers, civic actors, and healthcare practitioners will help to address the challenges and potentials presented in this book. This not only helps to harness the knowledge in the field of faith and society but may also generate needed resources, including funding for widespread work. Additionally, in the places cited in this book, what is needed is theologies that do not separate the private-religious and the public-secular. Such a dualistic split tends to disembody the world views of such places and makes the search for solutions harder. Hopefully, public theology (De Gruchy 1986; Forrester 1997; Trigg 2008), and particularly contextual theology through a decolonised lens can help address this.

References

Chesner, Anna, Lia Zografou (eds). (2013). *Creative Supervision Across Modalities: Theory and Applications for Therapists, Counsellors and Other Helping Professionals*. London: Jessica Kingsley Publishers.

De Gruchy, John W. (1986). "The Church and the Struggle for South Africa", *Theology Today*, 43(2): 229–243. doi:10.1177/004057368604300208.

Dwamena-Aboagye, Angela. (November 18, 2021). Conversation with Ruby Quantson Davis.

Forrester, Duncan B. (1997). *Christian Justice and Public Policy*. Cambridge: Cambridge University Press. doi:10.1017/CBO9780511605628.

Leach, Jane. (2007). "Pastoral Theology as Attention", *Contact*, 153(1), 19–32. doi: 10.1080/13520806.2007.11759074.

Leach, Jane. (2020). *A Charge to Keep, Reflective Supervision and the Renewal of Christian Leadership*. Nashville, TN: Wesley's Foundery Books.

Meyer, Birgit. (2011). "Going and Making Public. Some Reflections on Pentecostalism as Public Religion in Ghana", in Harri Englund (ed.), *Christianity and Public Culture in Africa*. Columbus, OH: Ohio University Press, 149–166.

Trigg, Roger. (2008). *Religion in Public Life: Must Faith Be Privatized?* Oxford: Oxford University Press.

INDEX

African Traditional Religion (ATR): belief in ancestral spirits within 52–53; practicing of, in Zimbabwe 45, 54; separation between religion and everyday life within, lack of 51–52; treatment of, by missionaries 100
agency 63–65, 104
Amnesty International 21
Apartheid, forgiveness and 79–80

Bernard of Clairvaux, Saint 105–106
Bourdieu, Pierre 13–15
Brooks, Cornell 81

Canadian residential boarding schools 100
Cathedral District Jax (CDJ) 28–30
charity *see* philanthropy
churches: agency of women in 63–65; as a civic gym 12, 27–29; effect of COVID-19 on 109–110; income of, worldwide 99; as a place of refuge for victims 59–63
citizens at the Center report, The 21
civic gym: religious groups as a 12, 27–29
CIVICUS 21

Civil Rights Movement, religion in the 16
collaboration, fostering of, need for 124–125
complementary production 91–92
consideration for the other, importance of 71–72
Convention on the Elimination of All Forms of Discrimination Against Women (CEDAW) 55
COVID-19: challenges related to 20, 21; effect of, on churches 108–110; effect of, on philanthropy 110–111
cross-fertilisation of ideas among religious groups 124

Declaration on the Elimination of Violence Against Women 38
deliberation: as a democratic practice 2–4, 24–25; in everyday politics 18–21, 88–91; framing of issues, importance of, for 23, 39, 56–58, 65, 89, 92–94, 127; gyae ma ne nka, application of, to 92–95; as a method of including marginalised voices 24, 26–27, 87, 126; recommendations and implications for 123–128; religious practices, need for, within 3–4, 27, 31, 94–95

deliberative guides, use of 20–21, 24
democratic approach to philanthropy, need for 111–114
democratic practices, promotion of gyae ma ne nka through 86–89
democratic spaces, need for creation of, within religious institutions 2–3, 87
Domestic Violence Act (2007) 49

epistemology xvii, 125
experience xii, xvii, 52, 85, 112, 115–116; centering 13, 40, 49; as epistemologically significant 14; listening to 50; lived xi, 6, 39, 93–94, 101, 110–111, 114; making space for 24; openness to 50; a place to process 83; value of 27

"feel for the game" 14–15, 20, 28, 110
feminist: lens 14; movements 19; readings xvii, 126; scholar 5; scholarship 63; theory 5, 14; theorist 63
forgiveness: cost of 82; politics of 79–80; as a process 84–85; *see also* gyae ma ne nka
framing of issues for deliberation, importance of 23, 39, 56–58, 65, 89, 92–94, 127
Freedom House 21

Gandhi, Mahatma 16
gender-based violence (GBV): addressing of, through deliberation 26, 37–38, 56–58, 63–66; African Traditional Religions perspective on 51–54; Christian perspectives on 44–51; as a human rights violation 39–40, 56; in Zimbabwe 41–44, 46, 59–63
Global Methodist Church 23–24
gyae ma ne nka: exploration of 70–76; promotion of, through democratic processes 86–92; reframing the process of 92–94; religious practices and 76–78; *see also* forgiveness

habitus, shaping of 14–15
Haval, Václav 32–33
hope 16, 18, 32–33, 48, 71, 78
human rights violation, gender-based violence as a 39–40, 56
hunger, addressing of 17

income of churches worldwide 99
Indigenous peoples, genocide of 15
intersectoral collaboration and learning, need for 124–125

Jean, Botham 81
Joshua, T.B. 16

Kyriarchal pyramid 105–106

leadership roles, prevention of women from holding 15–16
LGBTQ discrimination in the United Methodist Church 23
life-giving practices of religion 16–18

marginalised voices: hearing of, through deliberation 24, 126; suppression of, through gyae ma ne nka 73–74
mediation through gyae ma ne nka 76–78, 92–94
men's participation in finding solutions for GBV, importance of 55–56
Methodist church separation 23–24
missionaries, work of 15, 16, 100
Mugabe, Robert 60–61

naming and framing, importance of 29, 64, 92, 111–113
National Issues Forums Institute, The (NIFI) 20

ngozi 52–53
nodes 25, 27, 29–30

objectivity, governing of public debate by 2

pandemic *see* COVID-19
patriarchal systems: gyae ma ne nka, use of in 73–74; of Zimbabwe 40–44, 49–51, 56
philanthropy: addressing underlying issues behind, importance of 107–108, 126; in the Church 101–103; deliberative approach to, need for a 111–119; saviour complex and 103–106
politically motivated violence 41–42, 60–61
practices, religion and democracy as 13–18
proof-texting as a method of subjugation 47, 49

rape, politically motivated 41, 42–44, 60–62
redefining politics, need for 123
refuge, churches as a 59–63
refugees, plight of 17
religion: creation of democratic spaces within, need for 2–3; gyae ma ne nka within 76–78; harmful and life-giving practices within 15–18; problem of 21–25; separation of, from life, in African Traditional Religion 51–52
religious groups: as civic gyms 27–29; critical role of, in African society 87; cross-fertilisation of ideas among, need for 124
religious spaces, agency of women in 63–65
residential boarding schools, Canadian 100

saviour complex and the Church 103–106

scientific method, the 30–31
sexual violence in Zimbabwe 41–44, 45–46
sin, framing of gender-based violence as a 49
Start, Awareness, Support and Action (SASA) Faith in Action 50–51
suppression through gyae ma ne nka 73–75
sustainable development goals (SDGs) 5, 17, 61–62, 84, 124–125

theological appraisal and training, need for 127–128

Ubuntu 71, 80, 84–85
underlying issues behind philanthropic works, addressing of 107–108
United Methodist Church 23–24
Universal Declaration of Human Rights, The 38

victim blaming 47, 60
violence *see* gender-based violence; politically motivated violence; sexual violence in Zimbabwe

wealth inequality 17
womanist: readings xvii, 126; theories 5, 14
women: agency of, in religious spaces 63–65; as leaders in the Bible 48
women's voices, amplification of, need for 126
World Health Organization data on gender-based violence 39–40

Zimbabwe: initiatives to end gender-based violence in 50–51; patriarchal system of 40–44, 45–46, 56, 57

For Product Safety Concerns and Information please contact our EU representative GPSR@taylorandfrancis.com
Taylor & Francis Verlag GmbH, Kaufingerstraße 24, 80331 München, Germany

www.ingramcontent.com/pod-product-compliance
Lightning Source LLC
Chambersburg PA
CBHW050527170426
43201CB00013B/2121